FUTURE
PURPOSE

THE PLAYLIST TO DESIGN
A CAREER YOU LOVE

FUTURE
PURPOSE

JO ANN STREIFF HEROLD

Ripples Media

Published by Ripples Media
www.ripples.media

For more information: contact@ripples.media

First printing 2025

Book and cover design by Burtch Hunter

979-8-9859540-3-6 Paperback
979-8-9859540-5-0 Hardback
979-8-9859540-4-3 E-book

*Because the restaurant and hospitality industry has
given me so much, this book is dedicated to The Giving Kitchen,
a nonprofit whose mission is to help food service workers
in crisis. A big thank you to Jen Hidinger Kendrick,
Bryan Schroeder, Amy Crowell, Shelley Vincent,
and the team at The Giving Kitchen.*

*To my friends at McDonald's who have
been involved in my career at every step of the way,
and to my colleagues at Georgia State University for
making this chapter of my career the best yet.*

CONTENTS

FUTURE
PURPOSE

FINDING CAREER PASSION & PURPOSE

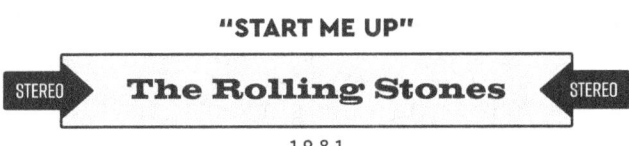

"START ME UP"

STEREO ▶ **The Rolling Stones** ◀ STEREO

1981

I WROTE this book to talk about the things I've learned over my thirty-year career. These are tips and advice, along with some hard knocks that I wish someone had shared with me.

In 2022, when I finished my first book, *Living on a Smile: 16 Ways to Live a Big Life and Lead with Love*, it was a love song to my friends, mentors, and family who helped me along the way to make life grand. To be clear, writing, editing, and launching a book is "no joke." Adam

Albrecht, a friend of mine and a fellow Ripples Media author, made the analogy that the publishing process is like running three separate marathons—with the writing, editing, and publishing phases each counting as a grueling endurance test. Publishing a book includes long hours, early mornings, and late nights, as well as occasional mild panic attacks and feelings of extreme vulnerability. You are sharing your deepest thoughts with a broad audience.

That said, I loved the process of launching a book. It was an exhilarating process and a way to help others, and I learned so much about myself along the way. The response to the book was very positive. I feel readers appreciate it when an author is authentic, transparent, and vulnerable. That is my promise to you.

Those who read my first book might wonder how this book is different from the first one. In short, this book focuses heavily on career fulfillment. *Living on a Smile* was written as a memoir with the objective of finding happiness within the context of not just your professional life, but also through your education, personal life, faith, and volunteerism. While I will certainly touch on those elements in this book, *Future Purpose* is written specifically as a manual for finding passion and purpose in your career. You can use it as a tool to guide you to find (or keep) a career you love. While no one is defined by their profession, finding meaning in your career often helps you realize happiness and fulfillment in other aspects of life as well.

Why is that?

Did you know that you'll spend about 25 percent of your adult life working? Think about the difficulty of finding happiness when you are doing something that is making you less-than-happy one quarter of the time. That is a lot of time, so, it's important to choose a career and job that makes you satisfied.

I hope to entertain, tell stories, and provide a guide to help design a career you love. One that passionately drives your purpose, values, and mission.

You will hear stories of others' careers and my own. I have interviewed people whom I admire to get their perspective. From these conversations, I hope to share valuable insights, lessons learned, and a richer understanding of their paths that led to success and fulfillment in a variety of fields. From unexpected pivots in the corporate world, to taking the jump to begin in a new industry, these stories reveal the importance of perseverance—and reminders to just enjoy the ride.

Throughout the book, I'll use the end of each chapter to create "key notes." This is a time for you to reflect, craft and create your plan to design and future-proof your career.

My thirty-year career has been shaped by personal passion, lots of crazy hours, experiences, going for it—and a lot of luck. I've sold lots of HoneyBaked hams, Arby's roast beef sandwiches, McDonald's fries, Interface carpet, and have taught young marketing students and ambitious MBA candidates along the way. These experiences have shaped me and I am so grateful for the people I've met through these opportunities.

I do what I love and love what I do. Sure, there have been bad days (they occur even in jobs you love), but thankfully, many more good days than bad.

You will see that there are two sections:

SIDE ONE: SETTING THE STAGE
SIDE TWO: TOOLS TO DESIGN YOUR CAREER

Within the sections, there are chapters of the book with song titles as sub-chapters. Music is a big part of my life, one of my passions and I try to incorporate it into my work life in ways such as meetings, conferences, and when I am jamming on a project. At the end of the chapter, I'll give you the backstory on the song I referenced that ties to the chapter. Writing this book continues to spur my love of music.

So much of my career has been spent in hospitality, as well as food and beverage. I love this industry. The food-service industry has given me so much in my career, including my time as a frontline worker at McDonald's, a regional marketing manager at Captain D's and Shoney's, a VP of Brand and Communications at Arby's Restaurant Group, CMO at The Honey Baked Ham Company (twice). It helped me land the CMO role at Interface, Inc. and recently in consulting roles with Focus Brands and creating new brands for private equity groups, like Crave Social Eatery.

At McDonald's, I learned that I love serving others and working for iconic brands. At Captain D's and Shoney's, I learned how to help franchise owners grow their businesses. I also learned a lot about navigating through some very tense conversations and having grace and grit. At Honey Baked Ham, I learned how to grow a brand, new product innovation, digital, and becoming a C-suite executive. At Interface, I learned what it means to work for a truly purpose- and mission-driven company. Finally, I loved my experience at Arby's and learned about how a big brand can work as an organization to do so much good together.

Today, I am working in higher education at Georgia State University and it brings me so much joy. I love working with highly intellectual people and being surrounded with young, smart, and curious students. My career really has come full circle and I am deeply grateful.

I hope this book serves as inspiration from the stories that are curated from others and from me. I also hope you use the pause to reflect on your own career and use the tool to design a career you love.

THE BACKSTORY

"Start Me Up" seemed like an appropriate opener for this book. It's widely known the song was written by Mick Jagger and Keith Richards, the Rolling Stone's primary songwriting duo. The song's backstory, though, is quite interesting. The song's origin dates back to the late 1970s when the Rolling Stones were working on their album *Some Girls* in 1978. At the time, "Start Me Up" was initially recorded as a reggae-influenced track with a different set of lyrics. However, the band wasn't entirely satisfied with the result, and the song was shelved.

Fast forward to 1981, as The Rolling Stones were preparing to release their *Tattoo You* album. They revisited the earlier recording of "Start Me Up" and decided to give it a rock 'n' roll makeover. The reggae elements were dropped, and the tempo was increased to create the energetic and catchy rock vibe that we know today.

This song was my high school anthem. I remain a huge Rolling Stones fan. It's an irreverent song and was a hit the year I started my first job at McDonald's.

SIDE ONE

SETTING THE STAGE

CHAPTER 1

ROLLING INTO A NEW POSITION

"JUMP"

STEREO **Van Halen** STEREO

1983

WHEN I rolled into an interview at McDonald's at sixteen years old in my silver Mustang, interviewing to be a STAR (store area representative), I never imagined it would create an entire career trajectory. Helping franchises grow became a common theme for me, along with loving being a part of iconic brands in the hospitality, food service, and sustainability business.

I always imagined I would live in New York and work in the advertising business. However, on a family vacation when I was in high school, I discovered Atlanta and fell in love with its beauty, culture, charm, and friendliness. I soon started my career here, with my husband and I landing in Atlanta and setting roots here after college.

Career has always been important to me. It's a way to help others, express my creativity, purpose, and passion. And while career is important, it's not what's most important to me. Family, health, service, travel, faith, and spirituality are integral and I work hard to integrate all of these priorities into my life.

So, with all of these interests, how does one find a career that accomplishes all of these things? From a career perspective, I have three areas I look for. It's a diagram that I use to make sure things are in check. Here are the three simple checkpoints I have:

1. Is this brand or business something I can get behind and stand for?

   ▸ Is this something I believe in?
   ▸ Does it have a purpose or a reason for being beyond just profits?

2. Do I like my boss?

   ▸ Does he or she have my back?
   ▸ Is this someone I can learn from?

3. Can we grow the brand or business?

- ▸ Are there enough resources to make an impact?
- ▸ Are the leaders willing to invest in the business?

IS THIS SOMETHING I CAN GET BEHIND?

IS THIS SOMETHING I BELIEVE IN?

IS THERE A PURPOSE BEYOND JUST PROFITS?

IS THIS SOMEONE I CAN LEARN FROM?

IS THE TEAM WILLING TO GROW THE BUSINESS?

DOES MY BOSS HAVE MY BACK?

ARE THERE ENOUGH RESOURCES TO MAKE AN IMPACT?

DO I LIKE MY BOSS?

CAN WE GROW THE BUSINESS?

Luckily for me, for the majority of my career, most of these areas have been in harmony. I've found that seeing things written out in front of you can provide clarity and contribute to a proactive approach to maintaining balance. When something is out of harmony, or I have the Sunday Scaries and a pit in my stomach, I go back to this diagram to diagnose where there might be an issue.

"SUGAR SUGAR"
The Archies • 1969

A headhunter called me when I was working as a regional marketing manager to ask if I would like to work at The Honey Baked Ham Company. I had never heard of them, but thought, what the heck? So, with my big hair and gold Honda, I rolled over to the Honey Baked Ham corporate office and interviewed. And, boy, did I interview! I had over twenty interviews with marketing, HR, leadership, and operations, landing the role as retail marketing manager.

I loved what I did and did what I loved. I was super fortunate to work with some pretty amazing people and have the opportunity to grow the brand and the business in a very compelling way. Together, the team launched new categories, including lunch, catering, and side dishes, as well as new platforms—web, order online, and pick up in-store. It also involved new promotions like more profitable marketing, done by leveraging brand advertising into the mix. In total, this would have been hundreds of millions of dollars over time.

The brand was so fun to be a part of, that I actually worked there twice. The first time for sixteen years and the latter stint for a little over five years.

I learned from my time at HoneyBaked that I loved working for brands where the consumer loved the product. Our team was very focused on excellence and delivering perfection for the customer and our field team. This is because the product was served at occasions that were so meaningful for the consumer—Christmas, Thanksgiving, birthdays, and funerals to name a few.

At HoneyBaked, we were highly cross-functional because we needed every department's expertise in order to deliver excellence. While it can be challenging to work with so many different points of view, I learned it made the effort so much better.

Working at HoneyBaked spurred my career and helped me bring skills and expertise to new roles, as well as grow in existing roles. And throughout my career, I've gone up and down and sideways on the ladder. Sometimes just to learn and build new skills or help out in a department who might have lost some leaders.

Through all the twists and turns, I've learned along the way that the career path isn't linear. An unexpected career interruption is often a blessing in disguise—even if it doesn't feel like that in the moment. While they absolutely force us outside our comfort zone, job changes and career transitions can be difficult, but they also present tremendous opportunities for personal growth.

Let me give an example from my own experience. If we look at the three question test I listed in the diagram earlier in this chapter, everything was in harmony the first two years I worked at Interface. I had a great boss, Dan Hendrix, who made sure I met all the key leaders in the company, understood our growth strategy, and was a mentor and great leader. I also really believed in Interface's purpose and mission. We then collaborated together to create values that were incorporated from the internal team and customers. Dan gave me a lot of authority to grow our product development, marketing, digital, and brand functions. It was definitely a highlight in my career.

Unfortunately for me, soon a new boss came in, and the leadership and culture changed. A new boss can trigger a new environment that makes it feel like an entirely new company. For me, what had been in harmony was suddenly now out of whack. These transitions are typical and can happen in any industry, but especially when you're working closely with upper leadership. Quite often, your happiness and fulfillment depends on mutual respect and trust with your superiors.

In my case, because the job did not provide the personal fulfillment that it had, it provided a serendipitous opportunity. I decided to move on, because I was traveling 90 percent of the time and working for a new boss that did not have my back. Too often, people stay in jobs that are unsatisfying because it's a familiar situation. This, however, is not an ideal way to find fulfillment. I left a very high-paying dream job without another one lined up because I knew it wasn't a good situation for my family.

As I look back on this decision, I have a lot of respect for my younger self for doing that. Was it scary? Yes. Was it the right decision? For sure!

Think about all the important moments in your life and the decisions that led up to them. Whether it was choosing a college, getting married, buying your first house—the list goes on. Most likely, in all of these cases, there was some underlying anxiety that came with this big decision and stretched you outside of your comfort zone. We have to be willing to live with some temporary nervousness and uncertainty in order to grow personally and find happiness.

Your career trajectory is no different. In order to find a fulfilling career that you love, you have to be willing to accept this. Too often, people stay in jobs they don't like because they have mortgages to pay and families to feed. While that need for security is understandable, if you want to find a career that you truly love, you often have to take some risks and accept some temporary uncertainty along the way.

To put it another way, rainbows only appear after a few thunderstorms.

JO ANN'S KEY NOTES

- Take the time to find a career you love.
- Don't stay in a job forever.
- A boss can make or break an ideal situation.

THE BACKSTORY

In high school, when I left McDonald's and went to be a server at Lil' Ray's, my tips and wages significantly increased. And in an outlier situation, I lived close to the Biloxi Coliseum during the height of the "hair bands." Van Halen was one of my favorite live bands to see and I love the song, "Jump." I've seen Van Halen perform live no less than twenty-five times.

"Jump" was the lead single from Van Halen's album

1984. The song was written by the band members, including Eddie Van Halen, David Lee Roth, Alex Van Halen, and Michael Anthony. Eddie Van Halen was known for his innovative guitar playing and hard-hitting rock and roll. However, "Jump" marked a departure from their traditional sound as it incorporated synthesizers more prominently, showcasing a more pop and keyboard-driven sound.

The lyrics are primarily straightforward and revolve around the idea of taking risks and seizing opportunities. The chorus repeats "jump" as a prompt to not hesitate and to dive headfirst into life's opportunities. And while "Start Me Up" was my high school anthem, "Jump" is my personal anthem for new ideas, new opportunities, new adventures, and fun and freedom. It's always on my playlist!

CHAPTER 2

THE NEXT
STEP AFTER
"GETTING QUIT"

"YOU DROPPED A BOMB ON ME"

STEREO ▶ **The Gap Band** ◀ STEREO

1982

"GOT QUIT" is a term coined by my long-time friend, Murray Weaver. Murray and I went to college together at Mississippi State. He and my husband Mark worked together at Frito Lay in Jackson, Mississippi, in the late 1980s. When someone was asked to leave their job, they would often say they "quit," when really they were asked to leave.

Mark and I have used this in our vernacular for years and we have passed on the term to others in a form of our own urban dictionary. People think the saying is funny and laugh because it's a way to add levity to a bad situation—until it happens to you and then it's not so funny.

Losing a job, especially when it isn't your idea, is a very stressful experience, and it can be similar to the grieving process. Denial and the feeling of shock and anger.

- ▸ Frustration and the reality of the loss sinks in.

- ▸ Bargaining and hoping to reverse the loss or change the circumstances.

- ▸ Sadness and a sense of loss are common during this stage.

- ▸ Acceptance whereby over time many people begin to accept the reality of the loss and find ways to move forward with hope and optimism.

"WHAT'S GOING ON?"
Marvin Gaye • 1971

I have seen all kinds of situations where someone has "gotten quit," seeing them experience all the stages. Sometimes a new leader can come in and bring in a new person. This happened to me one time and in retrospect, as hard as I tried early on to make it work, his decision was already predetermined. There was never anything I could have done to change his mind. And, while I shouldn't have been, I was shocked in the moment, and then went through all the stages of grief. Thankfully, I received a nice financial package that allowed me to lick my wounds and reflect on what would come next.

"SHAKE IT OFF"
Taylor Swift · 2014

Fortunately, I took my own medicine from the advice I've given when I've mentored and coached individuals who have had a similar experience losing a job. I have great empathy for anyone in this situation. A positive mindset and attitude, as well as encouraging friends and family, are key to getting through these situations.

It's also important to know the difference between your thoughts and your feelings.

Feelings are emotional experiences and represent your emotional response to a situation, thought, or external stimulus. Feelings include emotions like happiness, sadness, anger, fear, and joy.

Thoughts are cognitive processes that involve the mental activity of processing information, reasoning, problem-solving, and making judgments.

Guided by my own experience, here is a helpful process

I've found when dealing with adverse circumstances. They specifically relate to professional challenges, but can certainly apply to difficulties in other aspects of life as well.

▶ Acknowledge your feelings. They are real.

▶ Know that thoughts and feelings are distinct but interconnected aspects of our consciousness.

▶ And while you are acknowledging your feelings, fiercely guard your thoughts. Don't allow your thoughts to be hijacked with negative judgments.

▶ "Watch your thoughts; they become words. Watch your words; they become actions. Watch your actions; they become habits. Watch your habits; they become character. Watch your character; it becomes your destiny." — Frank Outlaw

▶ There is no timeline to progressing through the stages, but I've learned that the sooner one move on to acceptance, the quicker the next better thing will happen.

▶ Practice joy and gratitude. Only you can control your thoughts and when you feel those negative thoughts, smack them down and redirect them to something positive.

"LEAN ON ME"
Bill Withers • 1972

I personally went through these stages by acknowledging my feelings and recognizing what I was going through. I didn't try to sugarcoat it. I did a lot of journaling and prayed a lot.

During this time, I had a real crisis. My career was such an important part of my life and my identity. And deep down, I know this "stuff" happens, but it hadn't happened to me. And, it was hard to talk to others about it, so I worked hard to really take some time to reflect and learn from the experience.

I knew I'd need to have positive thoughts and believe that the best was yet to come. Every day I wrote down who or what I was grateful for and tried to do something kind for someone else. I also tried to be open to new opportunities and put myself in the position to find them. I became more active in some of the nonprofits I am involved with, especially Covenant House and Leadership Atlanta.

When you are going through these sort of transitions (especially one that you didn't seek out yourself), find activities outside of work to pour yourself into. For some, it may be nonprofits. For others, maybe it's a brand-new hobby, like learning to play tennis or running a marathon. Find outlets (aside from your job) that give you fulfillment and renewal. For me, it's connecting with friends and family and working with nonprofits.

Once I went through the stages, I started reaching out to people I'd worked with previously. A friend of mine, who had been through many transitions himself, encouraged me not to reach out to recruiters, but to pause, reflect, and not reflexively jump at the next gig. I took his advice and am so glad I did. As I reflect on this time in my life, I smile and feel grateful.

Life is not always rosy and personal success depends on rising above when things don't always turn out the way we thought they would.

After this happened, I was the CEO of my own business. I wrote and published an Amazon bestselling book, started a consulting business, received an Advanced Executive Coaching Certificate from Emory University, am a paid keynote speaker, and on the *Fast Company* Executive Board where I've had eight articles published at the time of this writing.

I've been a guest on countless podcasts, spoken at Zaxby's, McDonald's, and Georgia Pacific, moderated AMA meetings with amazing panelists, and served as an Executive in Residence at Georgia State University where I taught marketing to undergraduates and executive MBA students. I've had at least ten corporate clients my firm is working with to help them grow and thrive, and was the 2023 recipient of the AMA Marketer for Good.

I am now the Vice President for Marketing and Public Relations at Georgia State University and this has been the best chapter of them all.

I don't say all of this to be boastful or to brag. However, it's important to affirm your own journey and celebrate the wins that come after hardships. In the immediate throes of when I "got quit," I couldn't have imagined any of these accolades or accomplishments. I was caught up in my own loss and questioning my own identity, which was closely tied to work.

Yet all of these accolades and successes came out of that transition. I've learned through this painful process to have faith in myself and to have faith that things will all work out.

And, how do I feel about the boss who I "got quit" by? I feel appreciation and respect. I am genuinely rooting for his and the team's success, and cheering the team on. I know that while holding on to grudges may fuel some short-term motivation, having a chip on your shoulder fosters lingering resentment and is not a recommended path to happiness.

JO ANN'S KEY NOTES

- Be your own hype person.
- Have faith in yourself and the journey.
- Great successes come out of difficult transitions.

THE BACKSTORY

The song "You Dropped a Bomb on Me" by The Gap Band is rooted in the political and social climate of the early 1980s, as well as the band's own experiences and influences. The song was released in 1982 as part of their album *Gap Band IV*.

While the lyrics of the song are open to interpretation, listeners have interpreted "You Dropped a Bomb on Me" as a metaphor for the impact of a sudden and unexpected breakup or betrayal in a romantic relationship.

I love this song and danced to it at band parties at the Kappa Sig house when I was in college. The song is a blend of social commentary, musical innovation, and infectious energy that defined The Gap Band's music and contributed to their enduring popularity and why it's still on my playlist.

CHAPTER 3

VISUALIZE YOUR CAREER & LIFE

"I CAN SEE CLEARLY NOW"

STEREO ◄ **Johnny Nash** ► STEREO

1972

WAVE A magic wand and imagine what you'd like for your life to look like ten years from now. Five years from now. Three years from now. One month from now. Then write it down. And look at the long view as long as you can as you think through holistically how your career weaves into your overall life.

In the appendix, I include a Vision planning tool kit. I highly recommend writing out your plans and dreams, and spending time on creating a Vision Board.

For example:

▶ What does your family life look like?

  · Are you going on vacation?

  · Who's there?

▶ Where are you going? What's on your bucket list?

  · How are your relationships?

  · Are you having fun?

▶ How about health?

  · How often am I exercising? What is fun?

  · Am I getting my check ups?

▶ How about career and financial health?

  · Am I happy with my career?

  · What do I need to do to reach my financial goals?

▶ What are areas that bring me joy and happiness?

  · Who am I with?

  · What are we doing?

▶ What are the areas in spiritual life that are important?

  · Do I pray or meditate?

  · How can I live out my faith?

Vision boards are very powerful tools and can help make your dreams a reality.

It's definitely something many of my friends find valuable. Visualizing success and designing a life you love is relatively easy. However, I do know there are skeptics out there. And for those non-believers, I think there's great value in creating vision boards, and I'll explain why.

I love vision boards because real things happen when I put them out there. So, for my skeptics, try it and see what happens.

And here are a list of reasons why I believe it works:

Visualization
Vision boards help you visualize your goals and aspirations. When you see images and words that represent your dreams, it can reinforce your commitment and motivation to achieve them.

Clarity
Creating a vision board forces you to clarify what you truly want in life. It requires you to identify and prioritize your goals and desires, which can be a valuable exercise for personal growth.

Focus
By placing your vision board in a prominent place, you are

reminded daily of your goals. This constant visual reminder can help you stay focused on your objectives and make choices that align with them.

Positive Thinking

Creating a vision board encourages a positive mindset. You focus on what you want to achieve, and enhance your ability to manifest your desired outcomes.

Goal Setting

Vision boards can serve as a tool for goal-setting. When you break down your long-term goals into smaller, actionable steps, it becomes easier to track your progress and work towards them.

Motivation

Vision boards can be motivating. When you see your vision come to life, it can boost your enthusiasm and drive to work towards your goals.

Creative Outlet

It's fun and you can express yourself through images, colors, and words, making it an enjoyable and artistic way to set goals.

Accountability

Sharing your vision board with others or placing it in a social media space can create a sense of accountability. Others can support and encourage you in your journey.

Reflection

Over time, your vision board can serve as a reflection of your growth and accomplishments, reminding you of how far you've come.

In order to make my goals a reality, I keep it on my wall so that I can see it daily. I also have it as my screen saver and have shared it on LinkedIn and Facebook. We all want to live our best lives, and I am purposeful about reaching these heights.

Creating a vision board can be a fun and empowering activity that helps you stay focused on your goals and manifest your aspirations into reality. Whether or not you make a vision board, though, it is critical to lay out your dreams and goals, and visually plot out how you will get there.

Finally, another useful visioning tool comes from my friend and colleague from HoneyBaked, Dan McAleenan—the *Full Focus Planner*, by Michael Hyatt. I love this tool so much that I plan on becoming a certified trainer. I use it everyday and it's become my "go-to-resource" for making things happen. In my first book, *Living on a Smile*, I specifically outline more useful ways to utilize this planner and why it's been such a critical tool throughout my career.

Visualizing has helped me have so many things come true. For example, when I was twenty-seven years old, I put getting an MBA on my vision board. When I turned thirty I realized I hadn't made the plunge to do that. Because of the vision board, I marched down to Mercer and was able to meet with the dean. I enrolled that day and, boy, am I glad I did. The MBA gave me a seat at the C-Suite table because I had exposure to other functions, including accounting, legal, HR, IT and economics. I could speak the language! Fast forward, and I teach at the university level and am able to do so because I have a master's degree.

Visioning, especially with a vision board, can help crystallize your goals and ideas. I have had so many friends use them and are amazed at the power of them. I learned about the process when I was in Leadership Pasadena. Our facilitator had the entire class, all seventy of us, create and share our boards. This was twenty-five years ago and I was struck by the power of it.

Because visioning puts goals and ideas front and center, I've seen success in using this process in business as an approach for reaching new customers. It also promotes new ideas and initiatives, with teams as a key part of the process. For example, I used this process when I was at Arby's to help our culinary team create new products for new customers when we reimagined a new premium sandwich offering. The results were impressive, and helped grow the business in this segment.

JO ANN'S KEY NOTES

- Use a vision board for ideas at work, such as a new product or customer profile.
- Create a vision board and place it where you can see it daily.
- Make your visions a reality.

THE BACKSTORY

Johnny Nash was a Jamaican-American singer and songwriter. He released "I Can See Clearly Now" as a single in 1972 and it quickly became one of his signature songs. The song is known for its upbeat and optimistic lyrics, conveying a sense of renewal and hope.

"I Can See Clearly Now" was born out of this desire for positivity. Nash wrote the song himself, drawing inspiration from his own life and the idea of overcoming obstacles and challenges. The lyrics describe a person who has gone through difficult times but now sees a brighter future ahead, as if a fog has lifted and they can see clearly.

CHAPTER 4

PRIORITIZE WHAT'S IMPORTANT

"GIRL ON FIRE"

STEREO ▶ **Alicia Keys** ◀ STEREO

2012

THERE IS no road map for success. Often, it's a matter of choices you make and a lot of good luck along the way (Later on, we'll talk a little bit about the magic of showing up).

I do believe that prioritizing what's important to you is a gamechanger. This is true for family, health and wellness, spirituality, and career. Trust me, if you don't prioritize, what's urgent at work will always get in the way.

For me, I've learned to prioritize tasks that only I can do. I calendar the important things like family, faith, exercise, and having fun. In my career, here's how I try to allocate my time:

Marketing thought leadership, including listening to podcasts: **10 percent**

Writing about trends and culture: **10 percent**

Networking: **30 percent**

Getting the work done: **50 percent**

I have often found that you have to prioritize what's most important to you, your fulfillment, and your sense of identity. If you don't set aside time for it, it doesn't get done. There are always other competing requests and actions that can get in the way, and it's your job to make sure that the most important tasks get accomplished.

How do I personally do that? I use my *Full Focus Planner* to set goals and calendar to fill up on the top priorities, especially from the list above. I do this so that the big items are calendared. If I don't calendar items, other tasks get in the way, and the priority items can fall to the bottom of the priorities.

"I'M STILL STANDING"
Elton John • 1983

We all know that taking care of yourself is important for several reasons. It makes us better and more productive in all aspects of life. Here's a few of the why's for self-care:

Your Physical Health
Self-care helps maintain and improve your physical health and this includes eating well, exercising, and getting enough sleep to promote overall well-being.

Your Mental Health
This includes activities that reduce stress and anxiety. Taking time to relax, meditate, practice mindfulness, or engage in hobbies can help you feel more productive.

Your Emotional Well-Being

This involves recognizing and addressing your emotional needs. It can include setting boundaries and surrounding yourself with supportive relationships.

Your Productivity
When you take care of yourself, you are better equipped to handle challenges and be more productive. You have more energy, focus, and motivation to achieve your goals.

Your Resilience

Self-care helps build resilience. It allows you to cope with life's ups and downs more effectively. Resilience enables you to bounce back from setbacks and adapt to change.

Your Quality of Life

Practicing self-care leads to an improved quality of life. It means making time for activities and experiences that bring joy, fulfillment, and a sense of purpose.

Your Relationships

Taking care of yourself is essential for healthy relationships. When you prioritize self-care, you can give more and be present to others.

Your Prevention

Engaging in self-care can help prevent burnout and chronic health conditions. It's a proactive approach to maintaining your well-being.

Your Net Worth

Self-care reinforces your sense of self-worth and self-esteem. It sends the message that you deserve to be treated with kindness and respect, both by yourself and others.

Your Longevity

People who prioritize self-care often live longer, healthier lives. By taking steps to maintain your health and well-being, you increase your chances of enjoying a longer and more fulfilling life.

Throughout my career, I've had to prioritize multiple deliverables and priorities at the same time. Working for fast-moving consumer brands, there's never really a downtime. Time management is critical with these demanding roles. I learned to leverage several tools:

▸ I'd use Outlook for digital calendaring and would block out personal priorities, including attending my daughter's games or working out.

▸ And while I've tried mightily to move to 100 percent digital to prioritize and calendar items, I've learned that the paper approach is best for me for tasks. I use Full Focus or Covey to write out quarterly, monthly and daily goals and tasks. I love to check items off the list.

▸ In the evening I review the list for the day ahead so that I can wake up and hit the ground running. At night, I close out the list and move the items I wasn't able to complete to the next day and celebrate the items I was able to complete.

"BIG LIFE"
Ben Rector • 2018

Another visualization tool I love is called a Lifeline. I learned this through the executive coaching training at

Emory. Lifelines shows the highs and lows and can help create themes and ideas. It also shows the peaks and valleys over time.

The lifeline shows in a visual format levels of satisfaction over the years and can be a compelling way to show how events and triggers impact satisfaction and happiness.

In summary, self-care and prioritization is not a luxury; it's a fundamental aspect of a happy and healthy life and career. Self-care allows you to thrive personally and contribute positively to the world around you. And while the self-care and prioritization that I articulated above is a holistic approach to life, I do believe in bringing your whole self to your work and throughout your career.

Here's a tool I use to prioritize what's next. It's an exercise called "I am." After reading mine, try your own.

- I love my family and friends and they love me back.

- I am living a big, adventurous life filled with travel and hobbies, excited for each new day.

- I am a three-time Amazon bestselling author.

- I am in good shape and feel energized and healthy.

- I am a trusted advisor and coach to my clients.

- I am an award-winning marketer.

- I am giving back to my non-profit community.

- I am loved by my family and friends, and I love them deeply.

🔥

JO ANN'S KEY NOTES

- Do the things only you can do, like exercise and being happy.
- Create your own lifeline.
- Look for the patterns of when you had high points and low points to understand why.

THE BACKSTORY

"Girl on Fire" revolves around Alicia Keys' personal and artistic evolution. The song was co-written by Keys along with Jeff Bhasker, Salaam Remi, and Billy Squier. It was inspired by Alicia Keys' own experiences and emotions, particularly her journey of self-discovery and empowerment as a woman, mother, and an artist.

The song celebrates strength, resilience, and a sense of self-empowerment. The chorus, which repeats the phrase "She's just a girl, and she's on fire," serves as an anthem of self-confidence and determination.

"Girl on Fire" received positive reviews from music critics and became a commercial success. It reached high positions on various music charts and received several award nominations. The song also resonated with listeners for its uplifting and inspiring message.

It remains one of Alicia Keys' signature songs and has continued to inspire and empower audiences around the world. It represents a pivotal moment in her career, marking a transition towards more mature and meaningful themes in her music.

CHAPTER 5

SENDING
POSITIVE MESSAGES

"CHAMPAGNE JAM"

STEREO ▶ **Atlanta Rhythm Section** ◀ STEREO

1978

I RECENTLY received my Advanced Coaching Diploma from Emory and, during the certificate course, one area that we studied was neuroscience. The School of Medicine professors led this section of the course and it really opened my eyes to the importance of the messages we give ourselves and how they play into our confidence, strength, mood and overall well-being.

Sometimes we can be our own worst critic. We can tell ourselves stories that we repeat time and again, or ruminate over past mistakes. Often, these negative stories do not help us and can get us stuck or, even worse, set us back.

According to the Emory School of Medicine, neurogenesis is a process where the brain renews itself by generating 10,000 new neurons a day. Five thousand are daughter cells designed to keep the process going, whereas the other 5,000 go to where they are needed. *You* decide and can literally make up your mind to change your brain!

That being said, neuroplasticity is the process through which your brain self-organizes and decides how, when, and where it will use its structures and processes. So, here's the good news! You can train your brain and help to reorganize it.

During the program at Emory, we learned about the sections of the brain. And at the bottom of the head, near your neck, is the amygdala. This is your "homeland security" that is designed for survival. It often works fast with minimal data and is designed for the jungle. This is the area of the brain that prompts fight-or-flight responses and can get you in a world of trouble–especially in the corporate jungle.

Simply being aware of this helped me understand if and when my amygdala has been hijacked! There are simple methods to calm down the brain when you feel like your amygdala is being taken out of control.

When your amygdala is being hijacked, you may be experiencing heightened emotions and stress. The amygdala is responsible for processing emotions, particularly fear and anxiety. To soothe your mind in such situations, try the following techniques:

Deep Breathing

Take slow, deep breaths. This helps activate your body's relaxation response and can help calm your amygdala's response to stress.

Positive Self-Talk

Challenge negative thoughts and replace them with positive or rational ones. This can help reduce the anxiety that often accompanies amygdala activation.

Physical Activity

Engaging in physical activity, such as going for a walk or doing yoga, can release endorphins and reduce stress.

Social Support

Call someone or talk to a friend or family member about what you're experiencing. Sharing your emotions with someone you trust can provide relief.

Take a Break

If possible, remove yourself from the stressful situation for a short time to regain composure.

Journaling

Writing down your thoughts and feelings can help you process them and gain perspective on the situation.

And, according to Dan Coleman, *The Brain and Emotional Intelligence: New Insights*, the top five amygdala triggers in the workplace are:

1. Condescension and lack of respect

2. Being treated unfairly

3. Being unappreciated

4. Feeling that you're not being listened to or heard

5. Being held to unrealistic deadlines

And through the years, I've experienced all of these triggers. In this case, I'll use the example of a boss who displayed all the aforementioned triggers. To protect the identity of this boss, I'll call him Sam.

Sam is a highly intelligent person. He's one of those rare leaders who is quantitatively and qualitatively gifted. He understood the numbers, the stock price, the market, competitors, and internal and external capabilities. He is also a savvy marketer and has a deep understanding of the customer and what makes them tick. He could create plans and positioning and articulate these plans in a very compelling way.

So, you're probably wondering "Jo Ann, what's the problem?" Well, Sam was a narcissist who had a problem abusing alcohol. He had rage issues and would lash out at his employees and sometimes at me.

Here's what I did to protect myself, and my team, during this time period.

First, I tried to put myself in Sam's situation to better understand what might be going on with him. It could be a result of something that person is dealing with at home or at work. Or it could be that he had much deeper issues. Everyone has something they are dealing with, and sometimes it manifests into bad behavior at work.

Second, I took stock of the situation and wrote down what was going on. I've learned if I put it on paper, it helps me to analyze how to better handle the situation. It also made me feel better by simply journaling. I also talked to my husband, as well as a therapist, about what was happening.

Third, I learned that I must stand up for myself when there are specific situations. For example, my team and I presented our annual budget and plans to Sam. During a budget meeting, in front of a large group of people, Sam made some pretty disparaging remarks about the team and me. It hurt and embarrassed me, but most importantly, it hurt the team that worked on the project. I took time to reflect on the event and wrote down a script so that I could let him know the impact that his outburst had. From there, I scheduled a meeting and, in a very non-confrontational way, laid out why his actions were not OK.

Sam was not of the type of leader who was used to having a direct report stand up to him and the conversation really took him aback. He was extremely apologetic and promised he would be more aware and empathetic moving forward.

Fourth, if the situation is repeated and not sustainable, make actions to remedy what is happening. This could involve working within the organization to elevate what is happening with someone you trust within the organization. With the situation involving Sam, I alerted my HR partner and she helped me navigate the conversations within the organization.

Another tip is to work with an external mentor or coach. Someone who has your back and can help talk through the situation.

Fifth, know that nothing lasts forever and this too will pass. There are cultures or bosses that sometimes just aren't right. If that is the case, make plans to network and perhaps determine what is next and what is right for you. If it's really bad, and you can afford to do so, move on from the situation. And that is exactly what I did with the situation with Sam. I determined the situation I was dealing with was not going to be remedied and it was best for me to move on.

"LOVELY DAY"
Bill Withers • 1977

Having a routine and process for completing tasks, both at work and in your personal life, is so critical. For me, this structure gives me a daily framework for accomplishing the assignments I've committed to.

For me, positivity is essential for setting the tone for the day, and that starts first thing in the morning. When I wake up and think about the day, it sends positive thoughts to my brain about the day and literally says, "It's going to be a great day!" I wake up, make my bed, and try to do some form of exercise. From there I meditate, through either the Calm app or the Peloton app. This helps me set my intentions for the day before I dive into work. I also journal in the *Full Focus Planner* for a few minutes.

At work, I start with the minutia or the task I want to do least to get it out of the way. I do this so that I can enjoy the day and when I see people on the way to work, in the hall, at the reception desk or in meetings, I smile and try to build a rapport. It helps take some of the pressure off of stressful situations and makes the day more fun.

I am best in the mornings, and work to check the most challenging, difficult task off my list as soon as I can during the day. This could be tackling a hard project, creating a spreadsheet, or having a difficult conversation with a co-worker.

During the day, I take breaks and strive to get at least 5,000 steps per day. Even if it's a ten-minute break, I'll go outside and walk around the block so that I can get those steps. I've also learned not to sit at my desk (or in the car) and mow down lunch. Lunch is a time to collect myself and enjoy someone's company.

The afternoons are then filled with checking more things off the list, Zoom calls and getting projects moved forward. A perfect day also includes calling a friend and checking in.

In the evening, my husband and I will find something fun for dinner now that we are empty nesters. And now, an evening ritual for me is to look at what is scheduled for the next day and plan for it to be another great day!

Your daily process, of course, may not look like mine.

Exercising first thing in the morning may not be your preferred method of "setting the tone" for the day. Your most productive hours may be late at night. Whatever your process is, though, find a schedule that works for you and stick to it.

For me, that structure has allowed me to juggle demanding corporate jobs, family responsibilities, and non-profit commitments. Prioritization, which we touched on in the last chapter, is a huge component of productivity. Getting into a scheduled routine, which provides a consistent framework for those priorities, is the other half of it.

"JUST THE WAY YOU ARE"
Bruno Mars • 2010

In addition to establishing a consistent routine, find people who are your supporters. These are the friends who show up for you on the good days and the bad days.

One of my best friends, a former colleague at Honey-Baked and current business partner, is Maggie DeCan. She shows up for me at events, on social posts, and in everyday business settings. We talk about our positive strengths, how to complement and help each other. If I need to talk a situation through, I know Maggie is a text or a call away.

When Maggie and I worked together at HoneyBaked, we helped lead the brand and team through a very extensive rebranding. At the time, she was in charge of HR and I was in charge of marketing. Together, we led the team through a new brand promise. We brought out the insights from our customers, our leadership, our suppliers and most importantly, our team, to craft a premium and long-lasting position for the brand.

The work was embraced by the employees because of the way we approached, and executed the positioning. Because there was a great friendship between Maggie and I and so many of our cross functional partners, we were able to make a big difference for the business and help others enrich their careers.

My career has been so enriched by long-lasting friendships that I have made in all of the places that I have worked, from HoneyBaked to Interface to Arby's. Building close relationships with colleagues doesn't just provide social benefits, though. Having a support structure at work builds confidence and motivation, which in turn helps you do better work as an employee. It sounds simple, but one of the best ways to increase your own satisfaction at work is to seek out those friendships. It will have a positive impact on your social, and professional, life.

🔥

JO ANN'S KEY NOTES

- Set daily intentions. I want this day to be . . .
- Meditate using your favorite guided app.
- Journal as often as you can, and write your next chapter with you as the hero. Purchase a beautiful journal for your everyday thoughts and a notebook for thoughts that are frustrating. See which one gets more traction.

THE BACKSTORY

Atlanta Rhythm Section (ARS) was formed in Doraville, Georgia, in the early 1970s and gained recognition for their unique blend of rock, Southern rock, and pop music. The band's name itself, "Atlanta Rhythm Section," reflects their Southern roots.

"Champagne Jam" was released as the title track of their 1978 album of the same name. The song was written by Buddy Buie and Robert Nix, who were prominent figures in the Southern rock scene. The lyrics of the song describe a festive and lively atmosphere, with references to music, dancing, and of course, champagne. It embodies the party spirit and carefree attitude that was often associated with the rock and roll culture of the time. It's considered one of Atlanta Rhythm Section's signature songs and has contributed to their enduring popularity, especially among fans of Southern rock and classic rock music. I am a huge Southern rock fan and this song lives on all my playlists.

CHAPTER 6

NAVIGATING A CAREER CHANGE

"LEARNING TO FLY"

STEREO ► **Tom Petty**
and the Heartbreakers ◄ STEREO

1990

LEAVING HONEYBAKED the second time, I reflected deeply on how I wanted to proceed in the next stage of my career, and what would bring me the most fulfillment. I evaluated whether I wanted to land another big corporate CMO role or start my consulting and coaching practice. One of the areas I loved about being a leader is mentoring and coaching others.

As I was deciding what was next, I knew I wanted to coach, but wasn't sure if I needed to spend the time and money to get a coaching certificate. A coaching certificate is given after the student attends rigorous training on how to be a successful coach. You must also have over 100 hours of training by coaching others.

Being the researcher that I am, I spoke to over 100 people. I asked them whether or not I needed a coaching certificate in order to practice, or if it would be best to leverage my experience as a coach and mentor. In the end, I didn't land on a clear-cut answer, but the advice was invaluable.

Ultimately, I made the decision to get my advanced coaching diploma and I am so glad I did. There's a big difference between coaching and mentoring, and with the expert training from the Emory University professionals, I understand the difference.

Coaches and mentors both play valuable roles in guiding individuals toward personal or professional growth, but they differ in several key ways:

Focus and Expertise
- Coaches typically specialize in specific areas such as executive coaching, career coaching, or life coaching. They provide structured guidance and support to help clients set and achieve goals, develop skills, and overcome obstacles.

- Mentors, on the other hand, often have a broader scope of expertise and experience in a particular field or industry. They offer guidance, advice, and wisdom based on their own professional or personal journey, often focusing on career advancement, skill development, and networking.

Relationship Dynamics

- Coaching relationships are typically formal and structured, with defined goals and timelines. Coaches work with clients to identify objectives, create action plans, and track progress over time.

- Mentoring relationships are often more informal and based on mutual respect and trust. Mentors share their knowledge, experience, and insights with mentees, offering guidance and support as needed.

Purpose and Outcome

- Coaching is often goal-oriented, focusing on specific objectives such as career advancement, skill development, or personal growth. Coaches help clients identify obstacles, develop strategies, and achieve desired outcomes.

- Mentoring tends to be more relationship-focused, with the primary goal of supporting the mentee's overall development and success. Mentors provide guidance, encouragement, and perspective to help mentees navigate challenges and make informed decisions.

Formalization

- Coaching relationships are typically formalized through agreements or contracts outlining the scope of work, expectations, and confidentiality agreements. Coaches may work independently or as part of coaching organizations or consulting firms.

- Mentoring relationships may be formal or informal, depending on the context. Formal mentoring programs often pair individuals based on specific criteria, while informal mentoring relationships may develop organically through networking or shared interests.

While both coaching and mentoring involve guiding individuals toward growth and development, they differ in focus, relationship dynamics, purpose, and formalization. Coaches provide structured support to help clients achieve specific goals, while mentors offer guidance, advice, and wisdom based on their own experiences and expertise.

Now, I am able to leverage the coaching education in all interactions. I use it in my consulting practice and with my family and friends when they might have an issue, so that I can ask the right questions and lead them to realize the answer for themselves.

What is the lesson from this story? Very frequently, when we enter a period of career transition, we wrestle with that feeling of uncertainty, and uncertainty is hard. Especially for those of us who are goal-driven, we are always thinking about the next thing to accomplish or chase down. We want to find the answer to "what's next?"

However, sometimes a byproduct of this is that we rush into the first opportunity that seems like a fit, because it addresses that uncertainty and presents a clear path forward. When this happens, though, we don't give ourselves an opportunity to deeply reflect on what we want, not only in our career, but how our career fits into the other aspects of life. These times of transition are often the best time to deeply reflect on what truly makes us happy, removing the outside expectations that others have for us or that we place on ourselves.

In my case, I'd been a CMO for over 20 years and was very accomplished at it. That probably would have been the "traditional" path forward after my second stint at HoneyBaked. However, there was a part of me that also wanted to run my own consultancy. Also, I had always received fulfillment out of coaching and mentoring—I wanted to do more of that. Stopping to reflect on these other priorities and goals was critical in my discernment process. Now, I am full-time at Georgia State University and I love it. It brings together purpose and passion and helps the next generation grow.

When you are navigating career transitions of your own, let go of that need for certainty and reflect deeply on what truly makes you happy. Yes, it may mean that the period of uncertainty lasts a little longer, but you'll arrive at a decision that ultimately makes you happier. The "conventional" career choice quite often doesn't lead to the most personal growth.

In this next chapter, I'll outline ways to reflect more deeply and understand what drives you. As you navigate your next career transition, these are the questions that should guide your discernment process.

"I LOVE THIS GAME"
Jesse Itzler • 1996

One of my favorite books is *Atomic Habits: An Easy and Proven Way to Build Good Habits and Break Bad Ones* by James Clear. Clear talks about the science and psychology behind habit formation and offers practical strategies for making lasting changes in one's life.

Clear argues that small, incremental changes, or "atomic habits," can lead to significant improvements over time. In this book, there is a framework for understanding how habits work, and understanding how important reward is. Through this, he helps the reader understand the person they want to become.

I also follow Jesse Itzler, an entrepreneur, author, and rapper. He's got a great video called "How to Plan in 24 Minutes" and shares his quarterly and annual habits. It's on my bucket list one day to meet him and his awesome wife, Sara Blakely, founder of Spanx.

"LET'S GET IT STARTED"
The Black Eyed Peas · 2004

When I know there's a situation that needs to be enhanced or changed, I sometimes take the time to reflect and acknowledge what is going on. I'll work to dissect the issue whether it's at home, at work, health, or simply just being out of balance. Here are the steps I take:

Identify the Issue
The first step is to clearly identify the habit and what the issues are. Be specific about what you want to change and why you want to change it.

Set Smart Goals
Define clear and achievable goals for yourself. What do you want to accomplish with this change? Having a clear goal will give you something to work toward. Writing the steps to get to the goal has always helped me achieve it.

Understand the Trigger
Goals and habits often have triggers or cues that lead to

the behavior. As a result, it's crucial to understand what triggers you. For example, I get in doldrums on Mondays. Now, I plan something to anticipate on a Monday so I start to look forward to this day in the week.

Practice Positive Behavior
Instead of simply trying to eliminate the habit, replace it with a positive behavior. For example, if you want to find a new job, start reaching out to people you admire who have a role you'd like and ask for their advice.

Start Small
Break it into smaller, manageable steps. Don't try to change everything at once. Start with one aspect of your goal and work on that first. For example, when looking for a new job or career, start with updating LinkedIn to make sure your profile shines.

Use Positive Reinforcement
Reward yourself when you make progress or achieve your goals. This can help reinforce the new behavior. Write down how you'll celebrate when you reach your goal.

Stay Accountable
Share your goals with a friend or family member who can help keep you accountable. Having someone to support you can make a big difference. Sometimes I will post my goals on social media because it holds me accountable and lets others know also.

"ALL I DO IS WIN"
DJ Khaled • 2010

A young friend of mine, Kelly Strickland, was a student in my buyer behavior course at Georgia State University. She's a whip-smart go-getter and was looking for her first marketing job in the real world after she graduated, where she was also captain of the golf team.

Kelly eventually landed her dream job at Visa after a tenacious, and very strategic, job search, now serving as an associate for global digital partnerships. Specifically, Kelly tapped into her network, leveraged the expertise of professors, and the Georgia State career services center.

While Kelly is early in her career, these tips can be used for anyone who is seeking a career change.

"Applying to jobs can be intimidating, especially in a job market where it feels impossible to stand out," Kelly said. "After applying to over fifty jobs, over ten interviews, and two job offers later, these tips are what I found to be the best at getting your foot in the door!"

Utilize Your Network
People you have spoken to, met for coffee, or even connected with on LinkedIn are more likely to associate a positive connection with you. These small micro-connections help get your resume to the first round, spark

conversation around your experience, and ultimately give you a leg up. So send that LinkedIn message, make that phone call, or grab coffee! It is an easy way to stand out regardless of experience.

Stay Organized

My tried-and-true method of organization comes down to an interview outline. I have a five-page outline with the most common behavioral and technical questions that might be asked, paired with answers to each. This allows you to memorize your relevant experience, and practice how you want to verbalize it too.

Make Getting a Job Your Full-time Job

From August until December 2022, I applied to around fifty jobs and networked for each as much as I could. This was time-consuming and took up most of my evenings and weekends, especially interview prep. This dedication ensures the grind will pay off!

Get to Know Your Interviewer(s)

The more information you can find regarding your interviewer's background, the more the interview will feel like a conversation with an old friend. Find this information on LinkedIn, Google, or their company's website. As you are deciding what questions to ask your interviewer, this information will come into play. Ask worthy questions about their previous role, education, hobbies, etc., that will prove you did your homework. It will also make the conversation more personal, leaving a positive impression!

Don't forget, securing even a single job offer is a significant accomplishment worth celebrating. Despite what social media or LinkedIn might suggest, not everyone has multiple offers. Keep reminding yourself that you only need that ONE job offer to succeed!

♦

JO ANN'S KEY NOTES

- Develop your SMART goals (specific, measurable, achievable, relevant, and time-bound).
- Determine who you want to share your goals with.
- Determine where and how you want to celebrate your successes.

THE BACKSTORY

"Learning to Fly" was part of the Heartbreakers' 1991 album *Into the Great Wide Open*. The song was written by Tom Petty and his writing partner Jeff Lynne, who also co-produced the album.

Tom Petty often drew inspiration from his personal experiences and observations of life. "Learning to Fly" is no exception. The song reflects themes of personal growth, self-discovery, and the journey of life.

Tom Petty collaborated with Jeff Lynne on many songs throughout his career, and "Learning to Fly" was one of their most successful collaborations. The two had a strong creative partnership, which also extended to their work in the supergroup Traveling Wilburys.

The song was recorded in 1990 and released as a single in 1991. It became one of Tom Petty's most well-known and beloved songs. "Learning to Fly" achieved commercial success, reaching the top of the *Billboard* Mainstream Rock Tracks chart and making its way onto various charts worldwide.

The song remains a fan favorite and is a timeless message of self-discovery and resilience that has contributed to its enduring popularity. This song captures the essence of personal growth and the challenges one faces while navigating through life's journey. So, you can see that having fun with the approach and looking at what's next as a big, exciting puzzle can help you reach your goals.

CHAPTER 7

THE SERENDIPITY OF SHOWING UP

"WITH A LITTLE HELP FROM MY FRIENDS"

STEREO ▶ **Joe Cocker** ◀ STEREO

1969

SINCE THE pandemic, there are so many mixed emotions about going back into the office. While everyone is working harder than ever, we have loved our flexibility. In the meantime, CEOs want their employees back in the office as much as possible, and some are insisting on employees being at the office five days a week.

All the while, during the pandemic, new habits have formed as a result of our flexibility. From becoming more proficient in online collaboration platforms and tools, to creating dedicated home office spaces for work productivity, we have adapted to the shift of remote work. Often we like the change we personally create, and don't always enjoy the change others create for us.

For me, the hardest part of showing up is sometimes just getting there. I can think of a million reasons not to go to that dinner, to meet a client in their office, or attend a networking event. As an extrovert, I love being around people and teams and have missed the interaction with people. However, it's easier to just walk downstairs, hop on Zoom or Teams and go from meeting to meeting, all while never leaving my home office.

What I've learned, however, is that there is a serendipity to showing up. There can be fortunate, delightful, and almost magical things that can happen by seeing others in person. When I was consulting, I went to an evening networking event and met someone at the table who helped me secure a great speaking assignment from Georgia Pacific. I also received another consulting project from a fellow organization member.

These are opportunities that I certainly would not have received without attending the event. Even on video calls, in-person interactions foster connections that are hard to reproduce on Zoom or Teams. In my experience, the more I show up, the more unexpected and happy coincidences there are. As you grow in your career, you will find that the more events you attend and the more people you meet, the more serendipitous opportunities arise.

Here are my top seven steps for getting there (and I mean literally getting out of the house to be there, in-person):

Set Your Intentions
Visualize positive outcomes and optimistically look forward to being in-person.

Style and Smile
Wear something you love and smile. Along with your positive mindset, consider incorporating a touch of personal flair to your attire, whether that be a statement piece or a colorful accessory. You'll spark conversation, make new friends, and it will help your mood and outlook.

Show Up in Meetings and For Yourself
Participate in conversations or meetings in a meaningful way, whether that be professionally or personally. Also, spend time by yourself by taking breaks by taking a walk, grabbing a cup of coffee, or calling someone you enjoy talking to.

Stay Positive
Practice joy and gratitude. Beginning each day with a positive attitude, and remembering that you *get* to show

up, will bring a sense of gratitude. For instance, I keep a journal on the things I am grateful for and am glad to have the opportunity to show up for.

Show Respect and Be Kind

Know that you are asked to be in person, it's almost like an invitation to a VIP event. Your leaders are kindly asking for your presence and appreciate when their leaders foster positivity and commitment.

Satisfy Your Curiosity

Have fun, make new friends, and connect with your existing friends. It's an investment in you, but it also helps others have a positive mindset. Use humor and laugh a lot. Find the joy in the moment of connection.

Set Boundaries

By being there in-person and then being online at home, prioritizing your well-being is a must. No one wants to be "always on." Make sure you are engaging in mindful activities like getting enough sleep, eating well, and exercising.

INVEST IN YOURSELF

Investing time in showing up can help you position yourself for success. Build a rapport with your stakeholders—this can include your boss, collaborators, or peers. By inquiring about their weekend, family or things they love to do, you're opening the door to developing connections, and a positive environment. So, get there, show up, and have fun. Woody Allen said that "success is 90 percent about showing up" and I think he was on to something.

GUIDE FOR SHOWING UP

▶ Who do I want to see this year?

▶ Who do I want to see this month?

▶ Who do I want to see today?

▶ How do I want to show up?

♠

JO ANN'S KEY NOTES

- Map out and schedule events you want to go to in person.
- Wear something that makes you feel like a million bucks.
- Have fun, style, smile and remark over the good things that happen as a result of being there.

THE BACKSTORY

"A Little Help from My Friends" is a song originally written by John Lennon and Paul McCartney of The Beatles. The song is known for its soulful and powerful rendition by Joe Cocker.

Joe Cocker's version of the song became incredibly popular and is often considered one of his signature songs. His distinctive, raspy voice and emotional delivery added a unique flavor to the song, making it his own. My husband Mark and I saw Joe Cocker perform this song live in Las Vegas and became fast fans.

The song's lyrics reflect themes of friendship and support. It speaks to the idea that in times of trouble or difficulty, one can turn to their friends for help and comfort. Joe Cocker's rendition of the song is particularly memorable due to his passionate and soulful interpretation.

Cocker's performance of "A Little Help from My Friends" at the 1969 Woodstock Festival is especially famous and is often associated with the spirit of the 1960s counterculture. The song's enduring popularity has made it a classic in the world of rock and pop music, and it continues to be celebrated by fans and covered by various artists to this day.

CHAPTER 8

PRACTICES OF WILDLY SUCCESSFUL PEOPLE

"HAPPY"

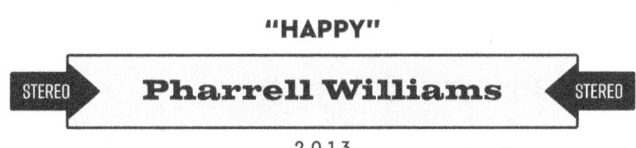

STEREO **Pharrell Williams** STEREO

2013

AS A MARKETING practitioner, and a former part-time marketing professor, I am always talking about the marketing P's with my students, co-workers, and clients. However, the marketing P's of latter years need a brand overhaul and should be reimagined as they have gotten a little stale and boring. As a reminder, the old marketing P's are product, place, price, and promotion.

In my role as a C-suite corporate marketing executive, as well as a community advocate and curious observer of so many amazing people, I have picked up common traits of many successful people. To build on their successful habits, I've created my own list of P's—traits of the successful people I admire that I'd like to share with you.

Brands are people, and here's the Top Ten P's and Practices of great people who lead strong brands and businesses:

Purpose and Platform

Great brands and leaders have a sense of "Purpose." They have excavated their reason for being and set forth a meaningful direction and purpose for their existence. This purpose is infused in all aspects of their life, including family, career, and community.

Brands and leaders also utilize their "Platform" to share the purpose behind the work, and give customers an inside look into their intentions. They are who they say they are and you see this in everything they do.

Passionate and Principled

"Passion" often leads to great success, because of one's dedication to their work and a "Principled" mindset. Leaders do what they love and they love what they do with ethical intentions. With that, these great leaders don't feel like they are working, because their work is their passion.

Planning and Pivot

Leaders manage their energy and try not to put themselves in situations that will deplete their energy. They manage their output and input. They acknowledge that life can deal out some hard realities, and their response to the situation is what matters.

Posse and People

Successful people have an amazing posse around them. They surround themselves with people who bring out the best in them and help them grow. They have friends and co-workers who are there for them on a good day and also there on their bad days. They know that no one is successful without the help of others.

Progress and Productivity

These successful people pack a lot into a day. Whether it's an early morning workout, a big presentation, or a pickleball game at night, they are always moving fast to get a lot done.

Personality and Play

Successful people work hard and play hard. They try to learn people's names and make meaningful connections. Two keys to effective leadership and success, they know that serious work can be completed without taking themselves too seriously.

Poise and Presentation

The successful people I love understand that being kind and grateful are always perfectly acceptable behaviors. They praise in public and give difficult feedback in private. They also know that humor is often used as a diffuser in stressful situations, and laughter is the best medicine.

Practice and Prep

Successful people know that what gets calendared gets prioritized. This can be for a big board presentation, a special toast for a loved one, or writing a thank you note to someone who has done something great. By giving others the tools of practice and preparation, they are set up for success. They push themselves, and others, to go beyond what was ever imagined.

Positivity and Praise

Positivity is a mindset and successful people know that being optimistic and praising others is motivating. They know there is no perfect process, and often pick others up through the journey and show them the way forward.

Pay It Forward and Promise

Successful people help others grow significantly. They are present for the people in their posse and work hard to pave the way forward for the next generation. They also identify and help the "up and comers" as they progress.

We all need principles, purpose, and positivity—sprinkled with a little pizazz—in our daily lives! So, from me to you, consider these our new leadership P's.

GUIDE TO BE A WILDLY SUCCESSFUL PERSON

▸ Identify which of the steps above resonate with you and you can weave it into your job and your life.

▸ Write down the people you believe follow the tenants in this chapter.

🔥

JO ANN'S KEY NOTES

- Wake up everyday with a positive mantra.
- Keep a grateful journal and take note of themes.
- Practice the top P's of wildly successful people and live a happy life!

THE BACKSTORY

"Happy" is a song by musician and producer Pharrell Williams. It was released as a single in November 2013 and was the theme song for the animated film *Despicable Me 2*. The song quickly became a massive hit, topping charts and receiving widespread acclaim for its infectious, catchy, and upbeat melody.

Pharrell Williams crafted "Happy" as a feel-good, funky pop track that featured his distinctive falsetto vocals. The song's lyrics revolve around the theme of happiness and feeling good, with lines like "Because I'm happy / Clap along if you feel like a room without a roof." The catchy chorus and upbeat tempo made it an instant hit, and it quickly became a popular anthem.

"Happy" won numerous awards, including the Grammy Award for Best Pop Solo Performance in 2015. Its success extended beyond the film and the music charts, as it became an anthem for positive thinking and a symbol of happiness in popular culture. The song's positive message and catchy tune have continued to resonate with people of all ages, making it a timeless feel-good song.

Fun side story here: my good friend Josh Martin headed up social media at Arby's during the 2015 Grammy Awards. During the Grammys, Pharrell was on stage with a hat similar to the brown fedora design, which became a trending topic on Twitter after he sported it.

Josh sent the tweet "heard around the world" saying, "Hey @Pharrell, can we have our hat back? #GRAMMYs." The tweet went viral!

Pharrell went on to put the hat on eBay, whereas Arby's bought it and gave the earnings to support his charity, From One Hand to Another. Pharrell tweeted thanks to the buyer Sunday, to which Arby's replied: "You're welcome. We're happy to support a great cause & get our hat back."

And this story makes me HAPPY!

CHAPTER 9

YOU BELONG
IN THE ROOM

"THE CLIMB"

Miley Cyrus

STEREO · STEREO

2 0 0 9

MUCH HAS been written about how men and women look at having a seat at the table differently. Men will take the front seat, take a lot of space and speak up. Whereas women will often take a back seat and try to take as little space as possible. Especially for the women reading this, it's so important to have confidence in yourself. It starts there. This chapter lays out ways to shift your mindset and believe you are meant to be there.

The first step is to positively see yourself in that company, in that room and at that table. No one else sees your issues, your flaws. The truth—harsh as it sounds—is that no one is thinking about you. Seriously, everyone else has their own journey and mostly they are in the same boat as you.

I've often been the only woman at the table, sometimes the only woman in the room of over 100 people. Mostly, I didn't think about it very often and knew I was in that room because of the skills and expertise I brought to the table.

When I was at Interface, I was the first woman to be in the C-suite. While it didn't really make a difference while at the boardroom table, I became very aware of being different from the rest of my teammates when we were traveling and at dinner and everyone was talking about golf or sports. As the only woman, I was often asked to create the PowerPoint or plan the holiday party. I often wondered why my male counterparts weren't asked to do the same thing. Hmmm.

It is widely known that men own the table. It doesn't matter their level, even male interns will scooch up to the table in a prime seat. Whereas, women, even senior level women, shy away from sitting at the big table. So, my advice to you is to own the table, sit next to leaders whom you respect. Know what will be on the agenda and prepare. Speak up and give factual insights as appropriate.

When you realize you are exactly where you are supposed to be at exactly the right time, take the power to read the room, engage in the conversation, determine how you can add your unique value and be a part of the company's growth plans moving forward.

And if you are ever speaking or working on a project and make a mistake, don't fixate on it. Acknowledge it, move on, move up, and keep going. Women often apologize a lot, bringing more attention to the mistake.

Also, if you are looking for a job and have an interview, know that you have every right to be in that room and have confidence in that belief. Look for companies or opportunities that align with your values and beliefs. Check out their website, LinkedIn, or Glassdoor and try to get to know people who work there.

Culture is key, especially since you will spend so many hours of your waking day interacting with the people you work with. The more you enjoy these people, the more likely you are to be successful.

◊

JO ANN'S KEY NOTES

- Sit confidently, speak up, and trust your value at the table.
- Shift your mindset, know the agenda, and contribute confidently.
- Choose workplaces aligned with your values for a more fulfilling career.

THE BACKSTORY

"The Climb" is a song performed by Miley Cyrus, and it was co-written by Jessi Alexander and Jon Mabe. The song was released in 2009 and became a big hit. It was featured in the soundtrack for the film *Hannah Montana: The Movie*, in which Miley Cyrus played her character Hannah Montana.

The backstory of "The Climb" revolves around its inclusion in the movie and its connection to the film's storyline. In *Hannah Montana: The Movie*, Miley Stewart (played by Miley Cyrus) faces personal and professional challenges as she navigates her dual life as a regular teenager and a famous pop star. The song serves as a pivotal moment in the film, where Miley's character reconnects with her roots and rediscovers her sense of self.

Lyrically, "The Climb" is about the journey of pursuing one's dreams and aspirations. It emphasizes that the path to success is not always easy and is filled with obstacles, but it's important to keep pushing forward and not give up. The song's uplifting message resonated with audiences, making it a favorite for motivational and inspirational contexts.

Miley Cyrus's heartfelt performance of "The Climb" in the movie and its subsequent release as a single contributed to its popularity. It became one of Miley's signature songs and remains a fan favorite. The song's enduring appeal lies in its universal theme of perseverance and hope, making it relatable to people facing their own challenges and striving to achieve their goals.

My daughter Lily and I used to watch Hannah Montana together and we were hooked. Lily even dressed up as Hannah Montana for Halloween one year.

I love Miley's grit, determination, and vulnerability and I was cheering loudly when she won her first Grammy for "Flowers."

CHAPTER 10

HAVING FRIENDS AT WORK

"THAT'S WHAT FRIENDS ARE FOR"

STEREO ▶ **Dionne Warwick** and Friends ◀ STEREO

1985

I RECENTLY read *Build the Life You Want* by Arthur Brooks, along with Oprah Winfrey. Brooks points out, "Happiness is a combination of enjoyment, satisfaction, and purpose. The 'four pillars' that support that trifecta are family, faith, friends, and work. Faith is anything transcendent that helps you escape the boring sitcom that is your life," he says.

One area I can't say enough good things about is having a best friend at work. I've always tried to find a best friend at work and I'd like to give a shout-out to mine who have been there through the years, including Maggie DeCan, Dan McAleenan, Ami Huff, Jim Hannan, Jenni Hong, Karen Anderson, Len van Popering, Hala Moddelmog, John Wells, Dan Hendrix, George Bandy, Mike Rotondo, Dr. Dawn Marie Kier, and my late, great partner, Debbie Domer.

Here's why:

Increased Job Satisfaction
Having a best friend at work can make your job more enjoyable. You have someone to share your daily experiences with, you can laugh, strategize and compare notes with them.

Improved Collaboration
Strong friendships at work can lead to better collaboration and teamwork. When you have a friend you trust and communicate well with, it's easier to work together effectively on projects and tasks.

Stress Reduction
Work can be stressful, and having a supportive friend at work can help you cope with stress. You can vent your frustrations, seek advice, and receive emotional support from your friend, which can improve your overall well-being.

Increased Productivity
When you have a friend at work, you may be more motivat-

ed to go to work and be productive. The social connection and camaraderie can boost your morale and motivation.

Career Advancement

Having a best friend at work can provide you with valuable insights and information about the company culture and politics. Your friend may also be a source of mentorship and guidance, which can help you advance in your career.

Enhanced Job Security

Close relationships at work can make you feel more connected to the organization. This sense of belonging can contribute to job security, as employers often value employees who are engaged and have strong relationships with their colleagues.

Better Work-Life Balance

A work best friend can help you maintain a healthy work-life balance. They may remind you to take breaks, encourage you to leave work on time, or even plan social activities outside of work to help you unwind.

Social and Happy Hour Support

Sometimes, work-related challenges can spill over into your personal life. Having a best friend at work can provide you with a source of social support that extends beyond the office walls.

As I enter this next chapter in my career, I look for ways to partner and collaborate with people I respect, can count on, and call my friend. I am partnering with Maggie DeCan, my former HoneyBaked colleague and friend. I often partner with Lisa Lilienthal, a long-time friend and collaborator. As of this writing, my mentor and friend Ken Bernhardt and I are partnering on working with an excellent nonprofit to help them grow.

Work-life is better when you have a bestie. So, plan lunches, coffees, and meetings with the people you have a great vibe with. It will be fun, rewarding, and will pay dividends through your lifelong career journey.

JO ANN'S KEY NOTES

Calendar time to build relationships with others.

Be yourself, there's only you.

Do epic things. Enjoy the journey.

THE BACKSTORY

The song, "That's What Friends Are For," was initially recorded by Rod Stewart in 1982 for the soundtrack of the film *Night Shift*. The most famous version was recorded by Dionne Warwick in 1985, featuring Elton John, Gladys

Knight, and Stevie Wonder. This rendition was produced as a charity single to raise funds for the American Foundation for AIDS Research (amfAR).

The song topped the Billboard Hot 100 chart and was a significant success worldwide. It won the Grammy Award for Best Pop Performance by a Duo or Group with Vocal and the Grammy Award for Song of the Year in 1986. The proceeds from the single raised millions of dollars for AIDS research and awareness. "That's What Friends Are For" became an anthem of friendship and support, highlighting the collaborative spirit of the music industry in addressing critical social issues. This version of the song is celebrated for its heartfelt lyrics and the iconic collaboration of some of the most prominent artists of the time.

CHAPTER 11

NEW SKILLS & WINNING HABITS

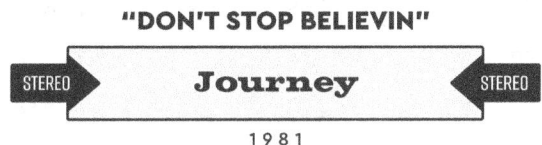

"DON'T STOP BELIEVIN"

STEREO **Journey** STEREO

1981

I TRY to add new skills to my arsenal as much as possible. In a world where technology advances rapidly and the needs of every job change quickly, being a lifelong learner is vital for career success.

More than just helping you stand out as a candidate in the market, though, mastering new skills have personal benefits too. They add to your overall well-being and boost confidence and productivity. Learning increases our own happiness and fulfillment.

Think about the last time you tried something new. This might have been a new hobby or sport (like tennis or pickleball), or even a new application or process at work (like making edits to a website). Regardless of the specific example, it was likely frustrating at the beginning, and you may have spent a number of hours learning the basics. Over time, though, as you practiced, think about the immense satisfaction that came with mastering that task.

While we often think about learning new things, especially at work, for the sake of productivity, this process brings immense satisfaction. It certainly builds confidence, but it also brings us happiness. It's a deeper sense of fulfillment, more than just a round of golf (which could also be a new skill to learn!) or a trip to the movies with friends.

Happy people know that:

▸ Defining and having strong values are key.

▸ Doing what you love and loving what you do make work and life more fun.

▸ Relationships are important.

▸ Being grateful improves your compassion and overall mental health.

▸ Serving others helps build altruism and human connections.

- Live your life with authenticity, transparency and integrity and you'll get to be your best self.

Look to try to gain new skills or add a positive habit every six weeks or so. They can be little things like adding in an evening ritual (like meditation or simply reviewing your calendar for the next day and prioritizing what you want to accomplish), or big things like becoming a certified coach. Some don't need to be very time consuming and many of these new skills can be life-changing!

Moira Vetter, a friend of mine, is the founder and CEO of Modo Modo Agency, an innovative advertising agency in Atlanta. She's grown the agency to a forty-person agency while creating a great culture with her employees and smart solutions for her clients. It's no wonder that she and her team win an award seemingly every fifteen days. Moira's team's mantra is to gain a new skill every day. On Fridays she and her team get together to review how they individually and collectively "Go Beyond the Ask." And what this means is that she and her team will go the extra mile for their clients.

GO THE EXTRA MILE

The frequency at which you should try to gain new skills or habits can vary depending on your personal goals, interests, and circumstances. Here are some factors to consider:

Career Goals

If you have specific career aspirations or want to advance in your current job, it's often advisable to continuously acquire new skills relevant to your field. This may involve ongoing learning and training. For example, I went back to school while I was working to get my MBA.

Personal Growth

Some people have a strong desire for personal growth and enjoy learning new things simply for the sake of expanding their knowledge and capabilities. In this case, you can set a regular schedule for skill acquisition based on your interests and things that could also enhance your career. Look for areas that drive your passion. For me, it's writing and I love to learn new things through articles and blogs I write.

Lifelong Learning

Lifelong learning is a concept that suggests learning should be a continuous process throughout your life. In this approach, you might dedicate time each week or month to acquiring new skills or knowledge in various areas. I love to read books and usually have three or four books I am skimming.

Project-Based Learning

Sometimes, gaining new skills is tied to specific projects or goals. You may learn new skills when needed to accomplish a particular task or project and then move on to the next skill when the situation arises. Raise your hand if there's a project you want me to be a part of and dive in and learn. This will be a win for you and a win for the organization. I recently received my advanced coaching certification and it's helped me coach others in team-based projects.

Adaptation to Change

In a rapidly changing world, staying adaptable and open to acquiring new skills is crucial. You may need to learn new skills more frequently to keep up with technological advancements or changes in your industry. For me, I am trying to leverage AI tools for brainstorming. I want to understand ways it can help me in my business and daily life.

Balance

It's essential to strike a balance between skill acquisition and applying those skills. Learning too many skills simultaneously without practical application can be counterproductive.

Did you know that Google offers free certifications through Coursera? These are great skills and legitimate certifications to put on your LinkedIn or resume that can help you stand out.

During my transition at Interface, I wanted to take the time to meet up with the people in my life who had helped me along the way. Because I traveled so much globally during my time there, I hadn't had a chance to keep up with some of my connections and wanted to re-kindle them.

In that time, I met with 100 or so friends. They were people who were bosses, mentors, and people I admired. It was rewarding to see these people, buy them lunch, and connect without any expectations of a favor.

When I started my own consultancy, I learned my time was less structured and I was out of balance, spending way too many hours working and not getting out and socializing with friends. I've had to re-calibrate how I spend my time to balance the work, along with relationships and exercise. It took scheduling and discipline to live this more balanced life while I was growing my new business.

Creating new habits can be challenging, but if you break it into small steps, with milestones and celebrations, it can be rewarding and fun.

♦

JO ANN'S KEY NOTES

- Read or listen to *Atomic Habits*, by James Clear, for ideas on how to make a habit stick.
- Map out your new skill agenda and plan.
- Find a friend or accountability partner to learn with you.

THE BACKSTORY

"Don't Stop Believin'" is a classic rock song by the American rock band Journey. It was written by members Steve Perry, Neal Schon, and Jonathan Cain. The song was released as a single in 1981 and is one of Journey's most iconic and enduring hits.

The backstory of "Don't Stop Believin'" is relatively straightforward, with the song's creation rooted in the collaboration of the band members. Steve Perry, the lead vocalist for Journey, came up with the melody and lyrics for the chorus, which he felt had a universal and uplifting message. Perry was inspired by the struggles and dreams of everyday people, and he wanted to create a song that would resonate with a broad audience.

Schon, the band's guitarist, and Cain, the keyboardist, played pivotal roles in shaping the song. They contributed to the music arrangement and co-wrote the verses, helping to craft the overall sound and structure of the song.

The song's lyrics reflect the idea of holding on to hope and never giving up on one's dreams and aspirations, even in the face of adversity. It tells the story of a small-town girl and a city boy who take a midnight train going anywhere, searching for something more in their lives. The song's message of perseverance and optimism struck a chord with listeners, making it a beloved anthem.

"Don't Stop Believin'" is played at Mississippi State games (#HailState) and is an anthem for many and lives on in rock music history.

CHAPTER 12

GET OUT OF YOUR COMFORT ZONE

"LIVE LIKE YOU WERE DYING"

STEREO | **Tim McGraw** | STEREO

2018

THE GRAPH on the next page is a fantastic visual to show the benefits of moving past your comfort zone. I look at it often and have even used an orange post-it note to plot where I am on my journey.

The growth zone is one of the most impactful stages. It's where we find our purpose, live our dreams, set new goals, and conquer objectives.

MOVING PAST
YOUR COMFORT ZONE

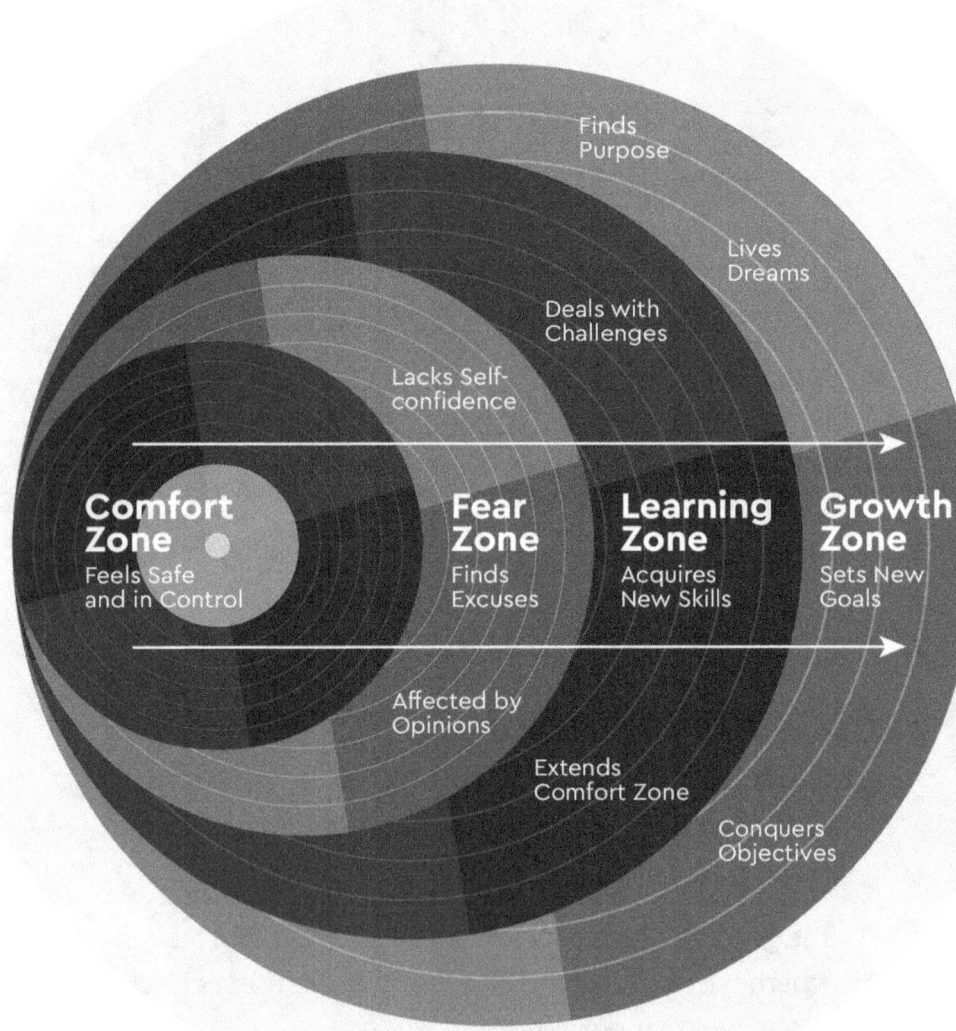

As I wrote this book, I asked some professional colleagues what they have done to grow to move out of their comfort zone and into the growth zone. The responses are broken into six themes.

1. MOVING TO AN UNCOMFORTABLE SPACE

"Go fast. The slower you go, the longer you feel scared. When you're going fast, you pick up momentum that propels you and the nerves turn into exhilaration."

Moira Vetter Modo Modo Agency

Moira owns Modo Modo Agency, a large business-to-business agency and marketing firm.

"Don't be afraid to make mistakes and not 'get it' right away—it takes time to get complex new things sometimes. Give yourself the grace to embody new capabilities and to have fun with the whole process."

Genevieve Bos Entrepreneur, Investor &
Advisor in Deep Tech Companies

Genevieve is an entrepreneur and advisor helping deep tech firms.

2. TECHNOLOGY & AI

"Last year I was serving in the capacity as a conference mentor and speaker for two AI pros. At the time, I knew nothing about AI. It was intimidating at first, but one of the most exhilarating experiences I've had in a while. Not only did I learn a ton about AI, I met two great people! My comfort zone expanded into a new technology."

Isabelle Albanese Consumer Truths

Isabelle is a longtime colleague who owns a consumer insights firm, Consumer Truths, which helps brands with research and strategy.

"Moving to a new city (NYC to Atlanta) and a lack of connections was an early area of moving out of the zone. Also I changed industries from music business to advertising. When I moved and changed industries, I was part of startups, which have high risk of failure, and I had to be resourceful. From there, I went back to college in my late thirties to learn more about a developing category in Sustainability Management, because I felt that companies were going to invest in ways to build and market cleaner and better.

"It's important to stay curious about emerging trends, which requires you to do research and test. For example, AI

is a new way of working and connecting with others."

Nick Schittone Chief Growth Officer, Hothouse, Inc.

Nick is the Chief Growth Officer at Hothouse, Inc., a growth-focused brand and marketing agency. He is also the immediate past president of AMA Atlanta.

"I am actively in the growth and learning zone while building our new software company powered by artificial intelligence, GAIM.AI. Being full-time in the corporate world while building a business on the side has revealed many learnings over the past couple years. Both personally and professionally, I have new goals, new objectives, and new dreams that take me out of my comfort zone but also get me one step closer to a future that I control.

"Work hard, listen more, be kind, surround yourself with good people, and stay vigilant in everything you do."

Zach Crain COO, GAIM Network

Zach, a former colleague of mine, is the former Omnichannel & Marketing Tech Transformation leader at The Honey Baked Ham Company and now COO GAIM Network and a best selling author.

3. TRY NEW HOBBIES & REMAIN CREATIVE

"When I was in my early twenties, I learned how to ski for the first time (both water and snow, but snow was much more terrifying for me). In my thirties, I learned how to drive a manual transmission, also terrifying. Those stand out because they are both huge risks in my brain if things go wrong: broken bones, massive injury, death... but you can choose to focus on that, or on the positives. I love to go fast. Skiing down an open hill in the tuck position to see just how fast I can go is one of the most thrilling things I have done. Does it suck to fall down? Yes. Do you feel embarrassed when you 'mess up' (also known as learning)? Yes. Is it worth it to keep pushing through to progress and growth? Yes!

"So that's an example of a physical fear and growth, but there is absolutely mental fear/growth and character-building too. Leadership is a huge one that has challenged me to step out of my comfort zone, learn what I don't know, make mistakes, and keep growing."

Ashley Jones Momento Foundation

Ashley, a fellow Ripples author, is the founder and CEO of Momento Foundation, whose purpose is to help people heal in grief.

"*Getting out of your comfort zone is always stressful but also filled with new opportunities. Right after COVID started I decided to write a historical fiction novel called* The Only Witness, *and it was well worth it. Not only have I become knowledgeable in history starting from the first century, but have developed a whole new cadre of friends around the world and have improved my writing skills.*"

Guy Powell ProRelevant

Guy is the owner of ProRelevant, a firm helping mid-tier brands improve their marketing strategies and ROI, and an author.

4. CONTINUAL LEARNING

"*After six years of account management split by two years of a full-time MBA, I switched into the creative department. No experience, no portfolio, no clue. Just a love for writing and a naïve belief that if I got a shot, I could do it. The shot came. The learning curve was insane. I had no idea how hard it would be. But a one-year experiment turned into a ten-year experience. Fear, learning, growth— barely a day of true comfort. But well worth it.*"

Evan Levy Fitzco

Evan is the CEO of Fitzco, an agency in Atlanta whose mission is to help clients sell more things to more people.

"I started a business and that put everything out of my comfort zone. It's difficult enough to continually stay relevant and leading edge throughout your career, then add the challenge of learning and leading with a second (new) set of skills required to run a company. That's a nod to all the fellow entrepreneurs out there!

"It's very similar to a manager who has been promoted because she or he does the technical job well and is now being asked to manage people. That requires a very different set of skills and doesn't come naturally to everyone."

Lisa Bigazzi Tilt Owner, Full Tilt

Lisa is the owner of Full Tilt, where she and her team work with business leaders to build their personal brand.

"Hire a direct report (for a crucial role) who thinks and operates so differently than you."

Ben Deutsch University of Georgia Adjunct Professor

Ben Deutsch is a board member, Leadership Atlanta alumni, mentor, and formerly a twenty-five-year executive at Coca Cola.

"Three things: (1) know when I've been happiest in my career. (2) know when I've created the most value in my career. (3) identified the commonalities when 1 and 2 coincided. When those common circumstances present themselves, even in what appear to be new or unfamiliar opportunities, I can be reasonably sure that leaping in will be OK."

Tom Daly Relevant Ventures

Tom is a marketer in Atlanta and the owner of Relevant Ventures, who helps brands with mobile, interactive and search marketing.

5. BEGIN IN A NEW JOB & CITY

"My biggest 'Growth Zone' was taking an international opportunity based in Europe for a few years. All of my colleagues in the U.S. were telling me I was making a mistake before I left. It wound up being the best learning experience of my entire life and it dramatically accelerated my career.

"I managed twenty-seven people in sixteen countries and learned more about the world in two years than I did in the previous forty years of my life. I highly encourage anyone seeking growth to move to another country or try to jump into a different industry at least once in their ca-

reer. Big thanks to Rob Boogaard for taking a chance on me and all of my wonderful colleagues from Interface who supported my journey."

David Gerson Interface

David Gerson and I worked together at Interface.

"For me, a big one was moving to Mexico in my early ca-reer to start the marketing function in our newly-opened Mexico City office. I was the first female US expat within a very large company, and had to navigate both country and company cultures.

Another would be changing industries during career transitions, from pharma to entertainment to telecom to the agency world and then to academia. I've had fun learning and adapting to all of the changes!"

Christina Steiner Emory University Marketing Executive

Christina is a great marketing mind at Emory.

6. GO BEYOND YOUR COMFORT ZONE

"Get the FUDD out!" No, really, that's what I had to do when I left my career in executive management with-in the food service industry to (finally) complete my book,

The Purposeful Growth Revolution: 4 Ways to Grow from Leader to Legacy Builder, and become a solopreneur. FUDD stands for Fear, Uncertainty, Doubt and Delay— common feelings we all go through when we want to bust out of our comfort zone and accomplish something extraordinary. It's been said, "A comfort zone is a beautiful place. But nothing ever grows there."

MARK MEARS Author and brand expert

Mark is an author of Leaf Growth Ventures and a brand expert.

Throughout my career, I've always prioritized surrounding myself with leaders whom I can learn and grow from. These stories were collected from friends, colleagues, and mentors I knew from all aspects of my career, whether that was through my employer (HoneyBaked, Interface), professional organizations (Leadership Atlanta, American Marketing Organization), or non-profits.

If you talk to any successful leader, they will inevitably mention how much they've been influenced by others in their careers. Quite often, a leader's management style was not in fact their own brainchild, but actually a process that they picked up from someone else. With this in mind, it's so important to be intentional about seeking out opportunities that foster growth and learning from others.

🔥

JO ANN'S KEY NOTES

- If you are in a rut, take a new route. Go on a retreat and break your habit.
- Use the comfort zone graph that is shown above. Put a dot on where you are now and where you want to be in six months.
- Put ideas and goals on your calendar and do it.

THE BACKSTORY

"Live Like You Were Dying" is a country song performed by singer Tim McGraw. The song was released in 2004 as the lead single from his album of the same name. The song was written by Tim Nichols and Craig Wiseman and tells a powerful and emotional story.

The backstory of the song revolves around the idea of living life to the fullest and cherishing every moment. It is inspired by a conversation that songwriter Tim Nichols had with his friend and fellow songwriter, Craig Wiseman. Nichols' friend shared a story about a man he knew who had been diagnosed with a terminal illness and given a short time to live.

This man, faced with the reality of his limited time left on Earth, didn't waste a moment. He embraced life with a newfound appreciation and made a list of things he wanted to do before he died. He went skydiving, Rocky Mountain climbing, and he even rode a bull. He also treated people around him with more kindness and love. The man's final days were filled with adventure, joy, and meaning.

This poignant story inspired Nichols and Wiseman to write "Live Like You Were Dying" as a way to convey the message of seizing the moment and making the most out of life. They wanted to encourage people to live without regrets and to appreciate every day, as if they were facing a life-altering diagnosis themselves.

McGraw's rendition of the song resonated deeply with listeners, becoming a massive hit in the country music world and crossing over into mainstream popularity. Its lyrics, along with McGraw's heartfelt delivery, struck a chord with people from all walks of life, reminding them of the importance of living in the present and making the most of their time.

"Live Like You Were Dying" received critical acclaim and won several awards, including the Grammy Award for Best Country Song in 2005. The song's emotional impact and universal message continue to make it a cherished and inspirational piece of music for many.

SIDE TWO

TOOLS TO DESIGN YOUR CAREER

CHAPTER 13

MASTERING A CAREER PIVOT

"FIGHT SONG"

STEREO | **Rachel Platten** | **STEREO**

2015

CHAPTER 12 had short bursts of insights about getting out of your comfort zone. This chapter digs deeper into stories of career changes and pivots.

For anyone who has been in the workplace for a while, you know that there will inevitably be a pivot and businesses, and you, will have to change and adjust. "The Pivot" happens and handling it with grit and grace can be a secret weapon.

I've always looked at my career as more of a game of checkers versus a game of chess. I realize there are some things that are out of my control and handling these situations by turning the proverbial lemons into lemonade has made my career fun. In this chapter, I solicit the wisdom of people I admire and respect and get their perspective.

"Have the humility to ask for help."

Teresa Caro
Business Clarity Coach and Founder of the Liminist

In 2022, Caro reached a crossroads in her career. After leading marketing teams for direct-to-consumer organizations, she had the option to seek out another leadership position in the advertising agency space, or start her own business. She ultimately chose to leverage her extensive executive experience into a new venture as an agency coach.

For Caro, she realized her expertise had evolved to a point where she could deliver more value as an external support system, guiding individuals, teams, and companies through transformative journeys.

"As friends of mine would expect, my approach to this career pivot was methodical and reflective," she said. "I recognized my value and the unique skills had developed over years of leading digital transformations for companies and mentoring leaders."

Caro, measured and analytical by nature, relied on her own self-reflection through the process, listening to what truly motivated her. "I learned the importance of embracing my own liminal state, recognizing it as an opportunity for growth rather than a barrier. This mindset shift allowed me to navigate the uncertainties of starting a new business with confidence and purpose. One of the keys to successfully navigating this change is remembering the power of humility and having the willingness to ask for help."

TERESA'S THREE KEY PIVOT POINTS

1. Embrace the Journey
"Understand that career changes are a process of self-discovery and growth. Be open to exploring new possibilities and be patient with yourself as you navigate through this transition."

2. Ask for Help
"Don't hesitate to seek guidance and support from your network. People are often willing to help if they know you need it. This can also include seeking professional advice (like an executive coach) to gain new perspectives and insights."

3. Communicate Effectively
"Clear communication with your current and future

stakeholders is crucial. Whether it's articulating your reasons for the change or negotiating new opportunities, effective communication can smooth the transition."

Teresa's Walk-up Song: "Happy" by Pharrell

"The Liminist's Core values include 'joy,' by "being self-less and putting other's successes first, joyful and taking a positive outlook on life and business," said Caro. "The lyrics have a tone of realism. Life is not perfect, yet I can (we can) choose to let it pull us down or we can choose to look for the gift and choose joy and happiness."

"When you choose to move, move with purpose."

Jeff Crow
Atlanta Chapter President, Founding Member of CMO Collaborative

For Crow, Coca-Cola was his dream job for much of his career. That changed, however, when the company went through a significant amount of change for the first time in his career. Suddenly, it no longer seemed like his forever place.

"It's a bit unsettling the first time that you come to that conclusion but in hindsight, it's also a sign of maturity and awareness that people change and evolve and sometimes the grass really is greener," he said.

On his way out, he reached out to colleagues and asked them what his strengths and weaknesses were. The feedback, much of it unexpected, was incredibly illuminating. Armed with new self-awareness, he expanded his network to focus on companies and people who were connected to areas where he felt he could make an impact.

JEFF'S THREE PIVOT POINTS

1. Change is unsettling, and that's OK

"It's unnerving but also freeing when you make a decision to leave a place that you've loved…where you're a known entity and you're valued. It's scary—the unknown always is."

2. Know when you've reached most of your potential

"Once I found my next gig and got situated, I had drinks with an old mentor from Coke. I expected to get a guilt trip, but instead he told me, 'I've been at the company twenty-three years, you were there nine. You learned 90 percent of what I know…the last 10 percent takes the most time…and it's not always worth it.' I've learned more and had a vastly wider level of experiences and successes than if I'd stayed where I was comfortable. For a while, I became the default resource for anyone in Coke marketing who was contemplating a similar move. It felt good to share that there was a whole other world out there!"

3. Make sure your change is intentional

"Be focused and don't jump ship just to jump ship. Understand what you want to do and then set a plan to get there. It's trite but ironic that most of us who spend so much time strategizing and planning in our business roles rarely take the time to do the same thing for our individual careers."

Jeff's Walk-up Song: "Family Table" by Zac Brown Band

"The best teams drive the best results and those teams are driven by the relationships made outside of the office," said Crow. "I also believe that everyone on the team should have a voice and that happens at a family table."

"Roadblocks will always be part of your career path."

Rachelle Kuramato
SVP of Brand and Content at BIP Capital

Rachelle has navigated a versatile career, from PR to freelance writer to footwear entrepreneur, brand agency owner, and now venture capital content and brand strategist. She attributes her education in writing and business as a springboard for the number of different roles she's held. She credits her father, who insisted she pair her literary degree with a business degree as well.

As she looks back on her career so far, there are three qualities she wants to be known for—confidence, depth, and kindness.

Ambition has been a key part of her success. She admitted that her ambition is so hardwired that it occasionally results in impatience when she's not seeing the results she wants. "I tend to allow a short time frame before expecting indications of progress. I often lose patience if a concept or opportunity seems more like dreaming than doing. Consequently, I've missed out on career prospects that ultimately became compelling and impactful.

"Forward motion is my state of being. I get genuinely excited, even antsy, when an opportunity emerges. Even if it's way out on the horizon, the glimmer of a chance to take on a challenge, contribute to something meaningful, join a group of brilliant people doing transformational things, and take another step in my career is irresistible."

RACHELLE'S THREE PIVOT POINTS

1. Roadblocks always exist

"The biggest in recent memory was hearing 'you are a bit much' from a colleague. It stung, and I could have allowed the perspective to knock me back. But solution-minded people don't see roadblocks as barricades. We see them as forks in the road. I looked around, took a brave turn, and ended up farther along in a fulfilling career journey than I could have imagined just a few years ago."

2. Always seek out mentors
"I will extol the value of career coaching to anyone who asks. I have found mentoring to be a constant undercurrent of support since my very first job. And I am an obsessive learner, always digging into concepts I can use to advance my career."

3. Annually assess your progress and priorities
"At the turn of every year, my husband Kenji and I go away for two days to focus on our priorities. During that time, as part of the larger initiative, I set professional Objectives and Key Results (OKRs) and take the time to plot the activities and milestones to reach them. That foundation allows me to stay focused and clear on how well I prioritize and progress toward my goals each month, week, and day. It's easy to dream about a career. Reaching the dream takes doing."

Rachelle's Walk-up Song: "Unstoppable" by Sia

"HALL OF FAME"
The Script ft. will.i.am · 2012

I am a tool geek. I love researching tools and apps that will help with goal-setting. Reaching goals requires careful planning, motivation, and the right tools to help you stay organized and focused. Here are some smart tools I recommend to help you crush your goals:

Goal Setting Apps

Trello: A project management tool that can help break down goals into tasks and track your progress visually.

Habit Tracking Apps

Streaks: An iOS app that encourages building and maintaining good habits by tracking streaks of consecutive days.

Note-Taking and Planning Tools

Evernote: A versatile note-taking app that allows you to capture and organize ideas, set reminders and plan goals.

Goal Tracking and Visualization Apps

HabitBull: A habit and goal tracking app that allows you to visualize your progress and celebrate your achievements.

Motivation and Inspiration

Pinterest: A platform where you can create vision boards and collect images, ideas, and quotes that inspire and motivate you.

Fitness and Health Goals

MyFitnessPal: A popular app for tracking your fitness and nutrition goals, helping you stay on top of your health and wellness objectives.

Online Courses and Learning Platforms

Coursera, edX, and Udemy: These platforms offer a wide range of courses to help you acquire new skills and knowledge, aligning with your goals.

Remember that while these tools can be valuable, the most important aspect of reaching your goals is your commitment, determination, and consistent effort. Choose the tools that work best for your specific needs and goals, and integrate them into a disciplined and focused approach toward achieving your desired outcomes.

♦

JO ANN'S KEY NOTES

- Determine what tool works best for you.
- Spend five minutes daily tracking progress.
- Watch your results and celebrate successes.

THE BACKSTORY

"Fight Song" was released as a single on February 19, 2015, and later included Rachel Platten's debut studio album *Wildfire*, both released in 2015.

The song became a commercial success and is known for its uplifting and empowering lyrics. Some of the notable lyrics from the song include:

"This is my fight song (Hey)
Take back my life song (Hey)
Prove I'm alright song (Hey, ha)
My power's turned on (Hey)
Starting right now, I'll be strong (Hey)
I'll play my fight song (Hey)
And I don't really care if nobody else believes (Hey)
'Cause I've still got a lot of fight left in me."

"Fight Song" resonated with me because it's an anthem of inner strength and perseverance, making it a very motivational song. I love it because it's badass and empowering.

CHAPTER 14

SHARING YOUR DREAMS

"BORN TO RUN"

STEREO ▶ **Bruce Springsteen** ◀ STEREO

1975

PEOPLE HELP other people rise up, and they will go up and down the ladder. Sometimes it's easy. Sometimes you have to climb and claw and grovel and laugh and cry! Climbing the ladder is hard work, so be kind to yourself.

While quite a bit of the "transition" part of finding a job happens online, there's no substitute for building strong relationships in all areas of your life. Networking can help you learn from others, gain mentors, and access opportunities. Plus, it's also fun and a great way to make new friends.

▸ Map out people you want to meet with or admire. Use a tracking sheet like Excel and list your conversations and any next steps. Start to follow them on LinkedIn and Facebook even if you haven't met them before. Like and comment on their posts.

▸ List the companies you want to work with. Include these on your spreadsheet also. Start to follow their accounts on LinkedIn and other social channels. You'll start to see posts regarding job openings and programs that they are working on.

   You can also check out their site and look at their vision, values, and purpose and how they treat their employees. Look at Glassdoor, ZipRecruiter, and Indeed to get a holistic view of the business.

▸ Use LinkedIn Premium. It will enable you to send direct messages to contacts within an organization. You'll also be able to see who's viewing your profile. LinkedIn is used by 77 percent of recruiters and 95 percent actively use it to search for candidates. According to LinkedIn, over 49 million people use the platform to search for jobs every week, and in every minute, six people get hired on LinkedIn.

▸ Leverage all the tools that LinkedIn offers, including having a strong About Section, a lot of followers, a professional photo, and good background. Also, ask former bosses, professors, and friends for recommendations. Showcase your work in the project section and leverage the skills area.

▸ That said, 60 percent of jobs are found through networking, not LinkedIn. So, leverage the power of your network. Ask your friends to introduce you to contacts that you'd like to meet. If you meet them in person, make it easy for them by meeting them near their office or home. Always write an email and a handwritten thank you note for their time.

▸ Get involved in trade organizations or volunteer with nonprofits, as they are powerful ways to connect with other like-minded people who can help on your search. These organic connections can offer invaluable insights, reinforce your drive and work ethic, and could even lead to job opportunities that might not be advertised elsewhere.

▸ Leverage your "Sphere of Influence." Friends, family, and coworkers are your most powerful influence and can help you identify prospects. Also, technology can help you connect.

Next, figure out how to be in the 1 percent Club. Most people think that being in the 1 percent club is about extreme wealth and lots of money. This is not what I am talking about. It's about surrounding yourself with the people who are at the top of their game. These are the positive people who make you laugh, have great insight, and are always growing.

For me, my circle is my eclectic group of marketers, authors, and community leaders. Those who are passionate about their craft and who love helping others.

Here's how I leverage my sphere of influence:

▶ Follow inspirational influencers: On LinkedIn, I follow influencers who have inspirational posts and insights. And I communicate with them. I have met many of them in person and become friends with them.

▶ Attend events with speakers you want to hear from or emulate. Meet the speaker after their talk and introduce yourself. Take notes and post your insights on LinkedIn or a blog and tag the speaker. Others will be inspired by these insights and you will send good vibes to the speaker who worked so hard to share their wisdom.

▶ Visualize how to grow your network to be a part of the 1 percent club: Once this happens, you'll be surprised by the inspiration they will provide you and the impact you can have on your area of the world and the community.

♦

JO ANN'S KEY NOTES

- Identify your first-level contacts. These are people who know and love you.
- Meet with them. Let them know what your dream career/job is. Ask for their help with ideas and contacts.
- Follow up, follow up, follow up.

THE BACKSTORY

Always on my playlist, this iconic classic-rock song known for its energetic and anthemic sound, capturing the spirit of youthful rebellion and the desire for freedom.

The backstory of the song revolves around Springsteen's own experiences growing up in New Jersey and his aspirations to break free from the constraints of his hometown. Springsteen had a turbulent relationship with his father and struggled with feelings of alienation. "Born to Run" reflects these themes of longing for escape and the open road.

The song's lyrics depict a couple longing to escape their mundane lives and embark on a journey together. It's a celebration of youth, freedom, and the pursuit of dreams. The driving rhythm, soaring melody, and Springsteen's impassioned vocals all contribute to the song's enduring appeal.

"Born to Run" became one of Bruce Springsteen's signature songs and a staple of his live performances. It has also been widely acclaimed by critics and has been recognized as one of the greatest rock songs of all time.

CHAPTER 15

PURPOSE, PLANNING, & PROMISE

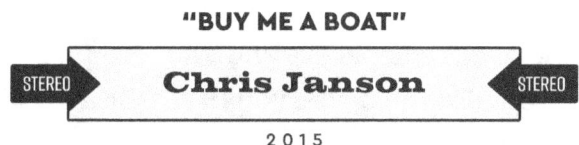

"BUY ME A BOAT"

STEREO **Chris Janson** STEREO

2015

JUST LIKE planning for a great vacation or a move, putting your career plan into motion takes strategy, planning, action, and follow up. Here are the steps I recommend.

Step 1

First, dig deep into your passion and purpose, following what you love to do and what you are good at. If you have not done that yet, take the time to do so.

Step 2

Now, write it out. Write your future bio and start with a story about yourself. LinkedIn will be your most valuable resource and use all the features that LinkedIn offers.

- Have a professional photo of yourself. Select a good background. It could be the company where you work now or a city skyline. Just make sure it's professional.

- Set the stage and give something memorable about yourself in the About area. For example, if you go to my LinkedIn, I wrote about my early experience at McDonald's.

- Give the reasons to believe and your proof points. These would be the places you have worked and the impact you have made.

- Write about your volunteer work and passions and give information that is personal. Perhaps this could be about your family, where you live, or interests.

Step 3

Get recommendations from former bosses, teammates, classmates. Recommendations will help you stand out from the others.

Step 4

Start to plot out your target companies or clients. The ways I determine my targets are:

- Look at the business chronicle in your area and determine the top companies in your targeted industry and write down your top twenty targets.

- Start following those companies on LinkedIn. You will learn a lot about their culture and strategies before talking to them. Look for mutual connections within those companies and try to meet them. Find out who their HR person is and send them your resume or LinkedIn.

- Check out their values, purpose, and learn more about their leaders. This will give you insights into their culture. Also, check out the company on Glassdoor. Culture and people are everything. You'll want to be associated with a company that has a positive culture and treats their employees, suppliers, and partners well.

Step 5

As much as it's a necessary evil, get your resume ready. Most resumes are filtered through technology, and it's not always a kind process. Look at job postings you aspire to have and make sure your resume (and LinkedIn) uses those keywords.

Here are the tips for a good resume

- Tailor your resume to the job and customize your resume for each job application by highlighting your skills, experiences, and achievements most relevant to the specific position.

- Use a clean and professional format. Choose a clear, easy-to-read font and a clean layout. Use bullet points to organize information and make it easier to scan.

- Include a strong summary or objective statement. Use this section to briefly summarize your experience, skills, and career goals. This can help grab the recruiter's attention and give them a quick overview of your qualifications.

- Highlight your achievements, instead of just listing job duties, focus on your accomplishments in each role. Use quantifiable achievements whenever possible to demonstrate the impact you've had in previous positions.

- Emphasize relevant skills and include a skills section that highlights the skills most relevant to the job you're applying for. This could include technical skills, soft skills, language proficiency, etc.

- Include keywords from the job description. Many companies use applicant tracking systems (ATS) to screen resumes. To increase your chances of getting past these systems, incorporate keywords from the job description into your resume.

- Quantify your achievements and whenever possible,

use numbers or percentages to quantify your accomplishments. This helps provide concrete evidence of your success and demonstrates your value to potential employers.

- Include relevant education and certifications. List your education, including any degrees earned, as well as relevant certifications or training programs completed.

- Keep it concise. Aim for a resume length of one to two pages, depending on your level of experience. Focus on including only the most relevant information and avoid including unnecessary details.

- Proofread carefully. Typos and grammatical errors make a negative impression on employers. Consider asking a friend or colleague to review it as well.

Step 6

Apply! You now have a strong LinkedIn presence and a good resume, so it's time to start applying to roles you might be interested in. But, finding the perfect next job can take time, so be patient and positive. It is a numbers game, so the more connections you make, the better your shots are. And while I have not personally done so, many are talking about using AI to tailor their resume for certain jobs so the HR system picks up their key words.

Remember, however, most opportunities come from other humans and connections, so leverage your networks inside the company.

Step 7
Now, get ready for that interview or pitch. Prepare and know about the business. Visit their website and if they sell a product, buy it. Know their competitors and where they sit in the marketplace.

Get ready for the interview. Here are some tips:

- Be ready for the "tell me about yourself" question. I use this in my *Living on a Smile* book, but here's a quick way to have this answer roll off your tongue.

- Know your strengths. I am a huge fan of the book, *Now Discover Your Strengths* by Marcus Buckingham. The book has a test you can take and it's good to have these ready to leverage when you get the questions about your strengths.

- You might be asked to answer situational questions. Be ready for these questions and write out your answers using the STAR approach (situation, time, actions, results). Some of these questions can be very tricky and being prepared will ensure you are able to answer the questions in a positive light. The interviewer wants to know how you think and how you will handle tough situations. A good book for situational questions is *High Impact Interview Questions* by Victoria A. Hoevenmeyer.

- Follow up and thank the interviewers by sending an email thank you and a handwritten thank you note to their office.

Step 8
You will spend a lot of time with the people you work with.

- Choose wisely.

- Make sure you have a good connection with your future boss. A boss's impact on engagement and whether you like your job is profound and can't be underestimated.

Step 9
Negotiating and knowing what you are worth are key to getting the right pay.

- Research average salary range for the role you are applying for.

- Ask the company what their salary range is for the role.

- Know what you are willing to accept, include vacation and perhaps time in the office versus hybrid.

- Only negotiate once during the process. It puts a bad

taste if the applicant keeps negotiating.

Step 10

The first ninety days are key to success.

- Have a beginners mindset. Go into it with the intent to learn and build relationships.

- Try to meet with the ten people you will be working with on a daily basis and get to know them. Ask them what their pain points are, and how you can help.

- Learn the business and read any research, reports and information that is available.

- One of my favorite books for a new job is *The First 90 Days: Proven Strategies for Getting Up to Speed Faster and Smarter* by Michael D. Watkins.

🔥

JO ANN'S KEY NOTES

- Leverage all aspects of LinkedIn. If you can afford it, purchase LinkedIn Premium.
- Research and target your dream companies.
- Set your plan in motion.

THE BACKSTORY

"Buy Me a Boat" is a popular country song released in 2015 by American artist Chris Janson. The backstory of "Buy Me a Boat" revolves around the theme of escapism and the desire for a better life. In the song, Janson sings about various material possessions he wishes he could afford, including a boat, a truck, and a Yeti cooler. These items symbolize a life of leisure and freedom from financial worries.

Despite its upbeat and humorous tone, "Buy Me a Boat" resonated with many listeners because it captured the sentiment of working-class individuals dreaming of a more comfortable existence. The song's catchy melody and relatable lyrics contributed to its commercial success and enduring popularity in the country music genre.

CHAPTER 16

STAY IN
THE DREAM JOB

"DOIN' THIS"

STEREO **Luke Combs** STEREO

2021

I AM currently in my dream role. So, this chapter applies to finding passion in any job or role so that you can continue designing the career you love.

Be fascinated with the business.

When I started my career at HoneyBaked, I realized how much I loved the business and the customers. I saw so many opportunities to grow the business into new areas and I'd often volunteer (or was "voluntold") to lead complex, multidisciplinary cross functional projects. It became my "sweet spot" and something I became quite skilled at doing. In the process, I tried to understand the problem and the pain points from every angle, including supply chain, finance, operation, IT, and HR.

Help others succeed.

This can be others on your team or within the organization. Look for ways to shine a positive light on them and give a helping hand when they need it. When I was at Interface, I had an amazing mentor, John Wells, who was President of the America's when I came into Interface from the food industry. John spent extra time teaching me about the flooring industry. I'll always be grateful for his mentorship.

Surround yourself with the best.

Bring the energy, bring the light. Be positive and have a great attitude, partnering with those who share your beliefs. There are going to be a lot of people in organizations who might be negative and want to spend time gossiping. Try to avoid that behavior and look for mentors and collaborators who are successful and achievement-oriented. Be someone who is so busy doing great things that you don't have time to lower yourself into negativity.

Drive the results and the growth.

Do your work on time and with excellence. Look for opportunities to improve the business overall and ask to be a part of the solution. When I was at Interface, I worked with the sales team to better understand their needs and where we had gaps in our product offering. Through this, we were able to give our product designer better direction on what products to offer. This grew our overall sales and results and made the company more profitable.

Be curious and lead your own development.

As much as we wish that others will help us with our development and training, it's often left up to the individual. Look for ways to continue to grow so you can add value in your career. For example, I asked my manager if HoneyBaked would pay for my MBA. My boss, Nancy Gibson, championed for me to go back, while working full time to get my masters. The MBA helped me in so many ways. It helped me be a better leader and executive. And I'll aways be grateful for that.

Keep building your tool chest.

Understand your strengths and continue to grow and flourish in these areas. For me, I love brand building and have been able to use the skills in my corporate work to help non-profits grow. I am on the board at Covenant House and also have several non-profits as clients.

Speak up, be unafraid, and have fun.

If you are following the advice listed above, you will know the business well at this point. Give ideas, show up for meetings prepared, and understand the agenda. Be the person who helps solve problems in a positive way. Be the one people go to when seeking advice and mentoring.

Make friends at work up and down the organization.

This includes with your bosses, your peers and the people who are more junior than you. Look for ways to help them grow and succeed. Go to the holiday party, play on the softball team and support any causes the company supports.

Dress for the job you want to have and dress for success.

Dressing well will give you confidence and show others that you are credible.

Your boss will be one of your keys to success in a job.

Work hard to build a rapport, have 1:1 meetings and understand what she/he needs to succeed. Work hard to create an easy working relationship (more to follow on chapter 17 on bosses).

Have your own external board of directors.

These are friends, former teachers, or coaches whom you admire. These are the people who you can talk to and get advice outside of your company. Choose people who will support you on a good day and a bad day and who are genuinely interested in your success. I have a formal and informal group of people whom I can call on when I run into an issue and need an external perspective.

♨

JO ANN'S KEY NOTES

- Be fascinated and curious.
- Be the one who decided to go for it and bring the light.
- It's not what you do, it's how you do it.

THE BACKSTORY

"Doin' This" by Luke Combs is a deeply personal song that reflects his journey as a country music artist. Released in 2021 as the lead single from his third studio album, *Growin' Up*, the song captures Luke Combs' passion for music and storytelling.

Combs revealed that the song was born out of a question he's often asked, "What would you be doing if you weren't a country music artist?" His answer has always been the same: he would still be singing and performing, whether it was for sold-out arenas or just a local bar. The song encapsulates his love for music as something he would pursue no matter the circumstances.

In the song, Combs highlights the simplicity of his passion. It's not about the fame, money, or accolades—it's about connecting with people through his music. This genuine love for what he does resonated with fans, making the song an anthem for those who follow their passions wholeheartedly.

CHAPTER 17

FIND THE BOSS OR CLIENT YOU LOVE

"THE BOSS"

STEREO **Diana Ross** STEREO

1979

OVER THE years, I have had many bosses and client partners. The majority of which I respected—they had my back and I had theirs. The best are those who take a genuine interest in you and want to see you succeed. As with any relationship, it takes two to tango. So, I really focused on having a great relationship with my boss or client, trying to understand where I could lend a hand, add value, build trust and help them and the business succeed.

I recently read a stat that surprised me in the book, *Well Being at Work*. It stated that, "Time with a Manager is the Worst Part of the Day for Employees," according to an approach called National Time Accounting that asks people detailed questions about their use of time throughout the day.

The question, and opportunity, becomes: *how do you flip that so that it's the best part of the day?* To assist in further understanding your current boss, *Harvard Business Review* has identified several types of bosses based on various leadership styles and behaviors. Here are some of the common types:

Visionary Leader
This type of boss is known for their ability to inspire and motivate their team with a clear vision for the future. They are often innovative and forward-thinking, able to articulate a compelling direction for the organization.

Coaching Leader
These bosses focus on developing their employees' skills and talents through mentorship and coaching. They provide guidance and support to help their team members reach their full potential.

Democratic Leader
Democratic bosses value input from their team members and involve them in decision-making processes. They en-

courage collaboration and strive to create a sense of ownership among their employees.

Authoritarian Leader

On the opposite end of the spectrum, authoritarian bosses tend to make decisions independently and expect strict obedience from their subordinates. They may be effective in situations requiring quick decision-making or in high-pressure environments, but can sometimes stifle creativity and innovation.

Laissez-Faire Leader

Laissez-faire bosses provide minimal guidance or direction to their team members, allowing them a high degree of autonomy. While this approach can foster independence and creativity, it may also lead to a lack of accountability and direction.

Transactional Leader

Transactional bosses focus on exchanges with their employees, such as rewards for good performance and punishments for poor performance. They often emphasize meeting specific goals and objectives.

These are just a few examples, and in reality, most bosses exhibit a combination of these traits to varying degrees depending on the situation and context.

In addition to the positive traits, there are several

traits that can contribute to making a bad boss. Here are some common ones:

Poor Communication Skills

Bad bosses often fail to communicate effectively with their team members, leading to misunderstandings, confusion, and frustration.

Micromanagement

Micromanaging bosses tend to excessively monitor and control their employees' work, undermining trust and autonomy.

Lack of Empathy

A lack of empathy can make a boss insensitive to their employees' needs, feelings, and challenges, leading to low morale and dissatisfaction.

Unfair Treatment

Bad bosses may play favorites, show bias, or treat employees unequally, creating a toxic work environment characterized by resentment and distrust.

Inconsistent or Arbitrary Decision-Making

Employees may struggle to understand the rationale behind their boss's decisions if they are inconsistent, arbitrary, or lacking in transparency.

Failure to Provide Feedback or Recognition

Employees need feedback and recognition to grow and feel

valued. Bad bosses may neglect to provide constructive feedback or acknowledge their employees' contributions.

Inflexibility

Bosses who are unwilling to adapt to changing circumstances or consider alternative viewpoints can hinder innovation and stifle work progress.

Poor Conflict Resolution Skills

Instead of addressing conflicts constructively, bad bosses may avoid them altogether or handle them in a confrontational or dismissive manner, exacerbating tensions within the team.

Failure to Set Clear Expectations

When expectations are unclear or constantly changing, employees may feel confused and unmotivated, leading to decreased productivity and job satisfaction.

Ego-driven Leadership

Bosses who prioritize their own interests, ego, or personal agenda over the well-being of their team and the organization can create a toxic and dysfunctional work environment.

Addressing these traits and cultivating positive leadership qualities can significantly improve a boss's effectiveness and the overall work environment. Also, it's important to realize that all bosses are not created equally. A good one is a gem, and a bad one can make or break your experience in your role.

♦

JO ANN'S KEY NOTES

- Develop a rapport with your boss or client to find out what success looks like and how you can help get them there.
- Understand that bosses are human.
- Embrace and learn from the good bosses and know when there is a bad one, this too will pass.

THE BACKSTORY

"The Boss" is a disco song recorded by Diana Ross. Released in 1979, it was the lead single from her album of the same name. The song was written and produced by Nickolas Ashford and Valerie Simpson, who were well-known for their work with Motown artists.

"The Boss" is characterized by its energetic disco beat and empowering lyrics. In the song, Ross sings about taking charge and being in control, both in her personal life and on the dance floor. The catchy chorus, with its repeated refrain of "Don't mess with the boss," became a signature part of the song.

The track was a commercial success, reaching the top of the Billboard Hot Dance Club Play chart and peaking at number 19 on the Billboard Hot 100 chart. It also became a staple of Ross's live performances and remains one of her most beloved songs.

Ross's performance of "The Boss" showcases her powerful vocals and dynamic stage presence, making it a standout in her extensive catalog of hits. The song's message of confidence and self-assurance continues to resonate with listeners, cementing its status as a classic disco anthem.

CHAPTER 18

STORYTELLING & PERSUASION

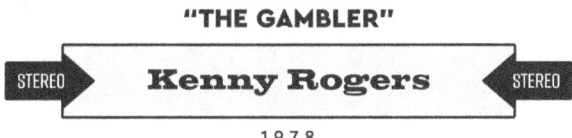

"THE GAMBLER"

STEREO ► **Kenny Rogers** ◄ STEREO

1978

HAVE YOU ever faced the scenario of preparing a big pitch or presentation for which your goal was to motivate your audience?

I certainly have, and through various experiences, I've discovered a set of strategies that can make all the difference with turning the audience tides in your favor. The insights you're about to take a read through have been instrumental in transforming presentations to impactful takeaways.

Prepare Your Material

Knowing your audience is key, so tailor your perspectives so that the presentation is relevant to the listeners. Good storytelling is personable, relatable, and thought-provoking. It can be shocking and scary, or humorous and surprising. Give the audience the invitation to marvel and wonder, and give them something to always remember.

Paint a Picture of What You Want the Audience to Take Away

Start with the beginning of your presentation in mind and develop your script. You will want to entertain them to draw them in, and importantly, have them visualize the benefits of your idea. Capture their attention from the beginning and start with a compelling hook, question, or surprising fact.

Plan Your Point of View

Plan your point of view by knowing your particular perspective, and show the audience what will happen if they adopt your plan. Focus on the meaning of what you are trying to say and then find the one word—that's right, the one word—that will encapsulate what you want to say. Then capture that story into an arc by having a powerful beginning, a compelling middle, and a strong close.

Put Your Words into Phrases

Put your words into phrases, and then select the one word that best captures your story. Include thoughts such as:

What does this one word mean we need? What does this one word mean we want? What does this one word show-case we know to be true? The one word could be "growth," "love," "transformation," "innovation," "connection," "possibilities," and so on.

Problem Solving is Key

Problem solving is key, and you can explain why the problem needs to be solved and how your vision can help. Use data and facts to tell the story, talk about the tensions of "What will happen if we don't solve this issue?" and then show the possibilities by using statements such as, "What if we were able to solve this?" and "The future will be bright when we have this."

Put Your Story Together

Put your story together in a way that is a smooth-flowing narrative, and think about the emotional connection you are trying to make between your audience and your story. Be clear and concise on what you want them to know, what you want them to do, and most importantly, how you want them to feel.

Presentation Matters

Presentation matters—and it's not just in the words you say. Imagine how you want to show up. Think through what props you will use. Limit PowerPoint to just a background, art, or brief bullet points to help listeners follow along, but use your story to convey your ideas. Think about your wardrobe and what you'll wear. My advice is to feel great in your style and comfortable in your clothes. The more confident you are in your style, the more confident of a speaker you become!

Practice, Practice, Practice

Record yourself and listen to your pitch. Find your voice, be clear, and say your story over and over until the words flow from you. Embrace the pause and use silence for effect. Think about your posture, standing tall and proud. Breathe and prepare for meaningful engagement, and know it's completely normal to feel anxiety or fear. But also know that you are very well prepared to make your pitch. Smile and have fun!

Present the Case and Make the Ask

Clearly outline the problem or opportunity, then provide compelling evidence and reasoning that emphasizes the significance of your pitch. Close with a great call to action and get the support you were looking for from your audience. This final push should energize the listeners and leave them with a clear understanding of their role in achieving the desired outcome.

Positivity Rules

Enjoy your accomplishments and know that you have made a difference by stating your point of view. By harnessing the power of your voice, you've not only conveyed your message effectively, but also inspired and influenced those around you. By using your voice to create a positive impact on yourself and others, you have created a space for meaningful, engaging dialogue.

As you move forward, let these experiences fuel your continued development and inspire you to approach future presentations with the same passion and confidence!

🔥

JO ANN'S KEY NOTES

- Know your audience. Have them at the edge of their seats.
- Give sound bites and ideas they'll remember.
- Make the ask and lead with persuasion.

THE BACKSTORY

"The Gambler," written by Don Schlitz and popularized by Kenny Rogers in 1978, is a great storytelling song due to its engaging narrative and relatable metaphor for life. The song tells the story of a chance encounter between the narrator and an experienced gambler on a train. Through the gambler's advice— "You've got to know when to hold 'em, know when to fold 'em, know when to walk away, and know when to run"—listeners receive valuable life lessons about decision-making and risk, all wrapped in a simple poker analogy. The vivid characters and setting, along with the song's clear structure, make it feel like a cinematic short story, drawing in the listener from the start.

What elevates the song further is its emotional depth and universal message. The gambler's wisdom speaks to the challenges we all face in navigating life's uncertainties, whether to persist, let go, or walk away. The advice resonates because everyone can relate to the moments where tough decisions are needed. The song's simple yet effective lyrics make its story easy to follow, allowing listeners to focus on the deeper meaning. This combination of memorable characters, engaging storytelling, and a powerful life lesson makes "The Gambler" a timeless classic.

CHAPTER 19

FUTURE-PROOF
YOUR CAREER

"TECHNOLOGIC"

STEREO ▶ **Daft Punk** ◀ STEREO

2 0 0 5

IT SEEMS like everyone is talking about AI. And while there are a lot of conversations about whether AI is good or bad, the bottom line is AI is here to stay. The technology's adoption is similar to the launch of personal computers in the 1980s. AI is another technological advance, and it's advantageous for people and businesses to embrace it.

Due to artificial intelligence giants like ChatGPT, it's predicted that generative AI will drive $4.3 trillion dollars in economic value. In any case, it's certain that AI will continue to be a part of business and our everyday personal life. In other words, how do we ensure that AI doesn't steal our careers out from under us? The answer is simple: Use AI to your advantage.

Here are the top ways to leverage AI:

Become Familiar With the Different Options of AI

- I'll use AI for idea starters to help spur the creative process. Some of the creative agencies I partner with use generative AI to automate the "business of marketing," especially in content creation, blogs, and personalization.

- Generative AI can be a powerful tool, it's great to see the first version versus the seventh version and watch the iterations. AI can also be used for research, design, animation, and ambient listening. It's always helping businesses with supply chain, automation, and business predictions.

80 percent of Businesses are Fast Followers

- Tech-y-type companies such as Shopify and Amazon are innovating in this area, it would be wise to watch them closely. Learn from the innovators about what's working and what's not.

- When testing AI with consumers, human oversight is key. It's important to understand your customer and look at any responses from their perspective. Have you ever applied for a job only to get a terse auto response? It would have been awesome for a person to have created a friendly response to someone who is interested in working with you.

When Using AI in Your Job, Pick Your Partners Well

- Partner selection requires heavy management oversight and humans are critical to success. Also, collaborate with cross-functional partners including legal, IT, and operations to create a vision and roadmap.

- While AI is skilled in knowing facts and information, it is still a digital system. There is always a possibility of incorrect data, and AI results are only as good as what is entered in your system. Collaborating with your team to have a human eye catch any mistakes will be a long-term benefit for your organization.

AI is Machine Learning

- Like a human, AI can make mistakes, not have all the correct information, and makes assumptions. Use AI as a tool, but also fact check and put your own fingerprint on anything you use from AI.

- It's taking the drudgery out of some businesses, and is wiping out some middle management roles. So, the first rule of thumb is to be good at your job and build relationships. Do things only you can do so that a machine doesn't take over!

Become a Student While Becoming an Expert

- I've used AI in low-stake areas, such as creating a LinkedIn post to see how it responds. And they have been eerily similar in voice and tone to posts I've created. Have fun with it, use it to create playlists, find great books, create a workout plan, brainstorm and for travel.

Successful innovators are always looking to learn more. Becoming a student of AI allows you to learn its many roles while increasing your own skills—such as creativity and problem-solving—that can be brought to the workforce. By adapting to this new space that includes AI, you don't risk being left behind and can learn all about this new tool.

AI is not leaving anytime soon. The more benefits it provides businesses, the less likely it will fade away into the shadows. But, as shown by reasons above, there are ways to utilize AI in your workspace. These are just a few reasons to leverage AI in your career, and dismissing them rather than adapting could hurt you more than help. It is just about finding the AI tools that make sense for you and your career.

🔥

JO ANN'S KEY NOTES

- AI is here to stay. Become familiar with it and learn how to leverage it.
- Become a user of new tools and share your learnings with others.
- Try AI for personal travel, ideation, and restaurant tips.

THE BACKSTORY

"Technologic" is a song by French electronic music duo Daft Punk, released in 2005, as the second single from their third studio album, *Human After All*. The track is distinctive for its repetitive robotic vocals and minimalist electronic beat, exemplifying Daft Punk's futuristic sound. The lyrics consist of a series of commands like "buy it, use it, break it, fix it," which are delivered through a speech synthesizer, giving them a mechanical, robotic feel. These phrases reflect the overwhelming presence of digital technology in modern life, a theme that was becoming increasingly relevant in the mid-2000s.

Musically, "Technologic" blends Daft Punk's signature mix of house, techno, and electro with a stripped-down but hard-hitting production style. The track is driven by a repetitive synth riff and simple beats, which create a hypnotic effect, drawing listeners into the song's futuristic and digital vibe. The song's accompanying music video, directed by Daft Punk themselves, features a robotic character miming the lyrics in a dark, industrial setting, further enhancing the song's commentary on technology's pervasive influence.

CHAPTER 20

FIND YOUR MOJO & LIVE YOUR DREAM

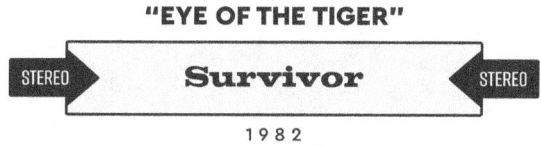

"EYE OF THE TIGER"

STEREO **Survivor** STEREO

1982

THIS CHAPTER features interviews from some of the most successful people I know. The leaders showcased here have had highly successful careers in multiple industries. They are all purpose-driven and help mentor the next generation.

FIND YOUR MOTIVATION AND RUN WITH IT

Paul Brown
Co-founder and CEO, Inspire Brands

Paul and I have known each other for years, and I had the privilege of working at Arby's Restaurant Group with Paul when he first took on the CEO role. Paul's career track has gone from data and tech, to marketing and sales, to founding and leading a global restaurant company.

Paul got a taste of the workforce by stepping into his first job in high school at McDonald's. While this role was primarily about learning how to operate restaurants and serve guests, he also began exploring potential career interests by working with data, analytics, and tech. Fresh off graduating from Georgia Tech with a business degree, Paul began working at Andersen Consulting, programming maintenance engineering systems for an airline client. From there, he has held partner and C-suite roles with McKinsey & Company, Expedia, Hilton, and Arby's. Paul then co-founded and became CEO of Inspire Brands, which was created following Arby's acquisition of Buffalo

Wild Wings, launching the company's vision of bringing together a portfolio of distinct, highly-valued brands.

The inspiration for Inspire stayed true to Paul's professional background—stemming from Arby's purpose statement, "Inspired Smiles Through Delicious Experiences." Having experienced pivotal transformations in the airline and hospitality industries, he started realizing similar patterns in the restaurant industry. The restaurant industry felt like a force for change, particularly driven by technology, and what technology could unlock for the business model. This created an opportunity to bring together and create a portfolio of individual brands that were very successful in their own right, but would be more effective collectively than they were individually, creating value for multiple stakeholders in the process.

But Paul ensured that at the heart of it all, Inspire and its team members embrace a purpose-driven culture and drive to be a part of something bigger. Since 2018, Paul and his leadership team have been building an environment for innovation, hustle, and a relentless focus on the guest experience.

PAUL'S THREE PIVOT POINTS

1. Be a part of what motivates you.

"We talk a lot about being here to do something that's

never been done before. We're here to build, we're here to change, that is our purpose, and we have a culture behind us that supports it. I think it's important to be very clear about what you are, what you aren't when talking to people about the decision to work for a company."

2. Don't rush the career journey.

"Obviously being motivated, working hard, trying to add value and get recognized is positive. Being impatient, trying to force the next move, taking the next step before you might be ready, is something to watch out for. Starting out, would I have done some things differently, sure. But ultimately the path I continued on has worked out very well, and a sense of patience can be attributed to that."

3. Use your experience as stepping stones.

"I think that the more you can build upon your previous experience in an analogous situation is really ideal. If I look at what my career is, it was taking what I learned in consulting and building on that in the situation with BCG and McKinsey, and then taking what I learned in the airline industry and applying it to travel, and then ultimately also did a decent amount of retail. And so, there were common threads there, right? I tried to carry that thread through as many similar situations as possible, and I'm always trying to build on them a bit."

Paul's Walk-up Song:
"Don't You (Forget About Me)" by Simple Minds

"I love it because it's just the imagery of it, right, the fist in the air, that movement. And, that was the same year that I graduated from high school, so I'm a product of the Brat Pack era. I like songs that make you feel just kind of happy and like anything can happen, anything is possible."

FIND PURPOSE AND PASSION IN YOUR CAREER

Hala Moddelmog
CEO, Woodruff Arts Center

Hala's career spans a variety of organizations and industries throughout the years. She has served on multiple boards, has a background in marketing and communications, and has held presidential roles at Arby's, Church's Chicken and Metro Atlanta Chamber. At the latter two, she was the first female president. She is currently the CEO of Woodruff Arts Center in Atlanta Alliance Theatre, Atlanta Symphony Orchestra, and High Museum of Art.

When reflecting on her own trajectory, she acknowledged the stress points of entering the workforce and becoming adjusted to having a heavier workload. But one point she emphasized is to not leave anything behind that you fear you're going to regret. She encourages leaders to remember that they can do more than they believe or think they can; what they're bringing to the party is enough.

"If you're really clear about who you are and what you want to do," she said, "don't start telling yourself no when you're young, because you're just going to look back and just think you are very much like that."

HALA'S THREE PIVOT POINTS

1. Find a purpose within your work.

"Church's Chicken was a pivotal moment. I was there for twelve and a half years and there was something about taking that little brand and knowing that those franchisees got what they deserved, making sure that the people in the field who were in the restaurant and who were overseeing restaurants got the respect that they deserved. It just felt like that we were really contributing something to society and we always felt that we were fulfilling a purpose for low-income people because they could get a family meal that was fresh chicken. We just felt that for a low amount of money we were giving them something that they could feel good about for their families."

2. Create as many positive moments as possible.

When I asked Hala what advice she would give her twenty-one year-old self, she responded, " I would tell myself that you can definitely have it all. Life is short, I didn't know what I thought would happen but I would just say, of course it's always nice to think that you could know at 21 that everything's going to be great. But, don't waste a minute. Burn it out, push it out, make it happen on every aspect of light that you possibly can."

3. Use gratefulness and happiness as a motivator.

"When I do live in that state of gratefulness and when I remind myself and think about it, that contributes to my happiness. If I had one goal it would be to live in a state of gratefulness because you're kinder to other people, you're kinder to yourself, and you're just a kinder person when you remember everything you have in this world."

Hala's Walk-up Song
"Respect" by Aretha Franklin

"For a woman my age who started out when there wasn't just automatic respect for women in business, I just love that song. I know it's a love song but it's about being a person in the universe and empowering me, I think that is brilliant."

BE PREPARED TO PIVOT

Daisy Tinsley Barnett
Founder and CEO, The Daisy Edit

Daisy's career started in media production. Watching Diane Sawyer on the evening news had a profound impact on her. Up until that point, most prominent journalist roles were held by men. Sawyer broke that mold in a smart, elegant, curious, and feminine matter.

Daisy majored in communications at Boston University, but her first internship showed her that the news wasn't exactly what she thought it would be. She found she was more interested in filming and editing, rather than being behind the camera. "I think I'm a little unusual in that I went to college for what I spent most of my career doing," she said. "So it was a decision based on identifying something I loved doing—creating media—combined with seeing someone who inspired me and who I felt represented me, and then trying it out and learning I needed to pivot a little."

Daisy has moved on to production and marketing

roles for technology companies like Adobe and Apple, and now is the co-founder and CEO of The Daisy Edit, a women's apparel company. The career change inspired her interest in style and helped women feel less overwhelmed in their fashion choices.

"After a year building a business and working one on one with clients I started to see how big a problem this was for so many women. They were overwhelmed with their wardrobes, most had gone through some sort of recent change—whether it was a life stage like menopause or a career change or just being in a slump since the pandemic. I then started hearing about AI and had an aha moment. What if I could scale what I was doing for my clients and build a styling service that leverages AI to help more women simplify their lives and feel great so they can focus on what matters to them?"

Throughout her career, though, the most valuable piece of advice came from her own mother. "I remember calling my mom when I was in my thirties, on my way home from work. Crying because my boss was horrible. I felt so trapped, at the time I thought my job was critical for my survival and identity. My mom calmly said, 'No job is worth feeling this sad about—just quit.' I learned about giving yourself permission, grace, and finding balance from my parents."

DAISY'S THREE PIVOT POINTS

1. If you're not sure about an opportunity, try it anyway.

"If you don't try you may have regret and if you do try and it doesn't work out, you'll still learn something. Give yourself permission to change your mind/quit and give it a try!"

2. Relationships are career currency.

"I like people and building friendships comes naturally to me. I never did this as a strategic career move but it really served me well."

3. There's no such thing as a straight path.

"Life happens, things are out of our control, we change, we grow. It's easy to connect the dots looking backwards and as you get further in your career you start to see how everything did move you towards your success—even if it didn't feel that way at the time."

Daisy's Walk-up Song
"That's Life" by Frank Sinatra

"The lyrics of the song remind me of the importance of resilience despite what life throws your way.

Each time I find myself
Flat on my face
I pick myself up and get
Back in the race

These lyrics resonate with me because I feel there are so many things we can't control. The human experience is something we sign up for the moment we are born and there are no guarantees. How we carry on in the face of adversity is.

BE IN TOUCH WITH YOUR OWN MOTIVATION

Monica McGurk
President, Glanbia Performance Nutrition (GPN) Americas

Like many undergrads, Monica didn't exactly have a clear career path after graduation. At first law school seemed like a possibility, but she later decided to get a job to pay down her student debt. She ended up in an operations role and subsequently at McKinsey, the well-known consulting firm, despite, by her own admission, having never opened a spreadsheet.

Her work in consulting led to a passion for the consumer industry—specifically food and beverage. Her work in the food and beverage area has led to roles at

Coca-Cola, Tyson, Kellogg, and Tropicana.

While McGurk has changed roles numerous times, it's always been with the goal of passion and fulfillment, rather than for the sake of new titles. "I've (always) stretched myself in new roles," she said. "I never have chased titles, as that is meaningless to me. It is more about the impact I can have and my own personal growth.

"One of the ways I pivoted was evaluating what was working between my professional and personal lives and making choices based on that. That included changing child care situations (I literally had at some point in my career every form of childcare imaginable), switching up clients when the travel load was not working, moving to new practices, taking alternative roles, even changing companies."

MONICA'S THREE PIVOT POINTS

1. Be in touch with your own ambition.

"Know yourself well enough to understand what will make you happy professionally, and take advice from others in that context."

2. Asking for help is a sign of strength, not weakness.

"Asking for help brings you closer and actually builds relationships. Nobody is ever offended when you ask them— quite the opposite! Especially as folks get into senior roles, it is increasingly rare, probably because others are intimidated or think you won't have time. But it is incredibly flattering. The worst thing that could happen is someone will say, 'I can't help you, but let me connect you with someone who can.'"

3. The more senior you are, the more your role changes.

"You need to be the one to open up the solution space, give room to voice the un-askable questions, tear down barriers and clear the way for the people you lead to do what they're great at. You're the one with the responsibility for helping the organization and every person you lead realize their own potential. You can have a unique impact on 'unsticking' what is stuck, cutting through bureaucracy."

Monica's Walk-up Song
"Short Skirt/Long Jacket" by Cake

"An oldie but a goodie. Some view this as a fantastical almost parody-like song about the search for the perfect woman who can do it all. Some view it as an ode to growing up and becoming responsible, or about the way women balance contradictory expectations. I love it in a more literal sense—the way the song depicts that femininity and bossdom aren't necessarily at odds—and I take as my mantra the idea of being the one 'who uses a machete to cut through red tape!'"

BE CONFIDENT IN YOUR ABILITIES

Stacey Tank
CEO, Bespoke Beauty Brands

Stacey and I got connected when we were both members of the chief communications officers group. I was at HoneyBaked Ham and she was at The Home Depot. Her career track has taken her from journalism to marketing, and now to lead executive.

Notably, Tank started as an intern at ESPN after majoring in broadcast journalism in college and eventually served as the president of The Home Depot's Installation Services division. She then moved to Amsterdam working for The Heineken Company as their Chief Transformation Officer. She now serves as the CEO for Bespoke Beauty Brands, which works with influencer entrepreneurs to build brands that represent creativity, inclusiveness, positivity, and self-acceptance.

STACEY'S THREE PIVOT POINTS

1. People are the most important factor for success.

"People are simply everything in life and in business. Getting the right folks in the right seats on the bus is essential. If you do that, most everything else solves itself."

2. Feedback fosters personal growth.

"One of my most important mentors and sponsors has been current Heineken CEO Dolf van den Brink. Dolf was my boss at Heineken when I joined the US team and later in Amsterdam. He always pushed me hard to be the best version of myself and was never afraid to hit me with tough love. This precipitated deep personal growth that I know wouldn't have happened in the same way without that coaching."

3. Be confident in your own leadership style.

"My first critical role model at work was Beth Comstock at General Electric, their first-ever female Vice Chair. She did things in her own way, with flair, and always ruffling some feathers (in a good way). This showed me that you need to be who you are and do what you feel is right, even if detractors say contrary things."

Stacey's walk-up Song
"Girl on Fire" by Alicia Keys

"When I was in my twenties, a C-suite executive at

General Electric (where I was working at the time) was describing me to someone who was about to meet me for the first time. I later heard that he said, 'That girl has fire.' It does resonate. I try to bring energy to everything I do!"

♠
JO ANN'S KEY NOTES

- Write your next chapter.
- Identify your "walk-up song."
- Find your jam!

THE BACKSTORY

"Eye of the Tiger," released in 1982, became a defining anthem of the 1980s and is synonymous with the spirit of perseverance and triumph. Survivor wrote the song specifically for the movie *Rocky III* after Sylvester Stallone approached the band, seeking a track that would capture the film's themes of resilience and overcoming the odds. Stallone initially wanted to use Queen's "Another One Bites the Dust," but when that fell through, he turned to Survivor, who saw the opportunity as a pivotal career moment. The band embraced the challenge, crafting a hard-hitting rock anthem that reflected Rocky Balboa's determination and fighting spirit.

The song's lyrics and driving rhythm capture the essence of an underdog's quest for victory, with lines about rising up to challenges and "staying hungry." The imagery of the "eye of the tiger" symbolizes focus, strength, and the will to succeed, mirroring Rocky's intense training and battles in the ring. With its raw energy, pounding guitar riffs, and inspiring lyrics, "Eye of the Tiger" resonated deeply with audiences, propelling it to the top of the charts and making it one of the most recognizable motivational songs in pop culture. It not only solidified Survivor's status in the music world but also became a timeless symbol of overcoming obstacles, both in the ring and in life.

DESIGNING A CAREER YOU LOVE

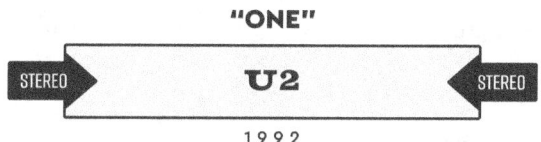

"ONE"

STEREO   U2   STEREO

1992

A CAREER is not simply about job titles or positions, but about creating a fulfilling life that aligns with your passions, purpose, and values. Like a carefully curated playlist, your career is composed of moments, choices, and experiences that, when combined, create the soundtrack of a life well-lived.

Careers, like life itself, are not linear. The twists and turns you face may at times seem like setbacks, but as many of the stories in this book have shown, they are often the very moments that lead to the greatest growth. From "getting quit" to mastering the art of the career pivot, from being the lone woman in the room, these moments are opportunities for reinvention, reflection, and rediscovery.

This book has been a joy to write. I've especially loved interviewing so many former bosses, mentors, and influencers who have modeled designing a career they love.

I love music and music has played a central part to helping me through my career. As such, here's a summary of the playlist. And when there's dark days or bad bosses, just turn on the jam and remember that tomorrow is another day.

Here's to the next track on your playlist—the best is yet to come!

JO JO'S PLAYLIST

START ME UP The Rolling Stones

JUMP Van Halen

YOU DROPPED A BOMB ON ME The Gap Band

I CAN SEE CLEARLY NOW Johnny Nash

GIRL ON FIRE Alicia Keys

CHAMPAGNE JAM Atlanta Rhythm Section

LEARNING TO FLY Tom Petty and the Heartbreakers

WITH A LITTLE HELP FROM MY FRIENDS Joe Cocker

HAPPY Pharrell Williams

THE CLIMB Miley Cyrus

THAT'S WHAT FRIENDS ARE FOR Dionne Warwick & Friends

DON'T STOP BELIEVIN' Journey

LIVE LIKE YOU WERE DYING Tim McGraw

FIGHT SONG Rachel Platten

BORN TO RUN Bruce Springsteen

BUY ME A BOAT Chris Janson

DOIN' THIS Luke Combs

THE BOSS Diana Ross

THE GAMBLER Kenny Rogers

TECHNOLOGIC Daft Punk

EYE OF THE TIGER Survivor

ONE U2

MORE ABOUT
THE GIVING KITCHEN

THIS IS my love song to the hospitality industry. I have received so much from this industry, it only feels right to shine some love and light back on it. The work that Jen Hidinger and Giving Kitchen does to support food service workers in crisis is incredible. Their unwavering commitment and compassion provide a lifeline to those in need, making a profound impact on so many lives. This dedication honors their vital contributions and celebrates the spirit of community and care that so strongly defines the hospitality industry.

Jen and her husband Ryan were presented the opportunity to be co-founders of Staplehouse, a restaurant focused on bringing together the community and fostering an uplifting spirit. The wheels started turning immediately, meeting with investors and banks, each step bringing Jen and Ryan closer to realizing their dream. This hard work has definitely paid for itself, with Staplehouse earning Bon Appétit magazine's Best New Restaurant in America in 2016 and a nomination as Best New Restaurant by the James Beard Foundation. However, they encountered setbacks and challenges, including Ryan's sudden illness—stage four gallbladder cancer. Immediately finding the support of close family and friends, Jen and Ryan decided to organize a fundraiser called Heidi – a short nickname for Ryan's last name.

Jen recalled the moment that she discussed with investors repurposing Staplehouse to a profit subsidiary of a nonprofit. When I asked Jen how that experience was, she shared that it was challenging, but also inspiring. She reflected on the profound shift in her life's direction centered around The Giving Kitchen, and how Staplehouse was a project close to her heart, but her true calling emerged in creating something larger than herself, that could make a lasting difference in people's lives. The realization of this broader purpose led her to devote herself fully to The Giving Kitchen, turning it into her second full-time commitment. Witnessing the organization grow under fierce leadership that is committed to direction and strategizing to accomplish the Giving Kitchen's goals has been nothing but inspiring for Jen.

When considering her vision for the Giving Kitchen, and the steps that need to happen in order to accomplish that vision, Jen expressed her desire for it to become the go-to place for both dining out and charitable giving. Considering this vision, she said, "it's a big effort but that's what I wanted, to be that place people just think of naturally when they think of food and a charity to give to." But, like many successful endeavors, steps must be taken first in order to fully accomplish that vision. Regarding fundraising efforts in 2024, Jen proudly mentioned their significant impact, having supported 20,000 food service workers—an increase of 40 percent over the past 18 months. She also highlighted the remarkable contributions of food service workers to the food industry and their incredible efforts to support the community.

Thinking back to her 21-year-old self, Jen reflected on what she deemed "one of the most remarkable decades of my life." A piece of advice she'd give herself, that I'm sure would resonate with many young adults, is that hardships are inevitable and can feel overwhelming at times, but they do not define you. Learning to lean on and trust the resources and supportive people around you is key to overcoming those hardships. Jen also emphasized the importance of understanding that there are individuals who genuinely want to see you succeed and thrive, and believe in the inherent goodness of people. Even during moments of uncertainty about career paths or opportunities, she would encourage embracing exceptional opportunities when they arise.

Coming from a founder's perspective, Jen encourages those still searching for their passion and dream role to focus on what they want their purpose to be. Then once you find it, you have to ask yourself, "How do I build on this, and continue to my purpose and passion?"

For Jen, this came very easily. Her goal has always been to give a megaphone and a voice to those within the food service industry, and provide a platform. Starting from her own experience as a frontline worker at McDonald's and Captain D's, then moving into her roles within Staplehouse and Giving Kitchen alongside Ryan, and continuing to build Giving Kitchen's legacy in his honor, Jen has a deep gratitude for this industry and asks herself, "how do we uplift our industry?" Giving Kitchen embodies the perfect avenue for giving back, supporting frontline workers and elevating the industry as a whole. As a close friend, I'm thrilled to support Giving Kitchen in any way I can, and be a cheerleader for their years of success to come.

Jen's Walk-up Song
"Thank You" by Boyz II Men

Because it's full of gratitude.

A BIG SHOUT OUT AND THANKS

WRITING A BOOK is never a solo endeavor—it is a labor of love, supported by those who inspire, challenge, and encourage along the way. As I bring this book to life, my heart overflows with gratitude for the people who have played a role in this journey.

First and foremost, I thank my family. To my husband Mark, your unwavering belief in me and your constant encouragement make all the difference. Your patience, humor, and love sustain me, and I am forever grateful for your presence by my side. To my parents, Mike and Marilyn, modeled for my family, Mike and Blake, what it's like to have a big career, parent, serve your community and be a good friend and neighbor.

I love my daughter Lily so much. She brings such joy, enthusiasm, and wisdom to all. I hope she loves her career and purpose as much as I have.

And to my sweet posse, Karyn Froseth, Stacy Gryboski, and Julie Bowerman, you have been my cheerleaders, my sounding boards, and my champions. Whether through thoughtful conversations, encouraging texts, or simply sharing a laugh during stressful times, you have helped me stay the course. Your belief in me has fueled my passion to share these words with the world.

A special thank you to my colleagues and mentors, past and present. To my team at Georgia State University, and to President Brian Blake, your dedication and passion for excellence inspire me every day. I am honored to work alongside you in shaping the next generation of leaders.

To my former colleagues from Honey Baked Ham, Arby's, Interface, McDonald's, and all the places where I have had the privilege to lead and learn—thank you for the lessons, challenges, and friendships that have shaped me. Your influence is woven throughout these pages.

To my dear friends in the marketing and business communities, I am so grateful for the wisdom, collaboration, and inspiration you bring into my life. Special thanks to Ken Bernhardt, whose mentorship has been invaluable; Randy Hain, whose guidance has been a source of strength; and Maggie DeCan, whose leadership and friendship continue to be a gift.

To my incredible literary team, Andrew Vogel, Jeff Hilimire, DMF and the Ripples team, thank you for helping shape my vision into reality. To the readers—thank you for picking up this book and joining me on this journey. Whether you are a leader, an entrepreneur, a dreamer, or someone seeking inspiration, I hope these words resonate with you and encourage you to live and lead with love. Your time and attention are gifts, and I do not take them lightly.

Finally, I give thanks to the faith that guides and sustains me. I believe that we are all here to make a positive impact, and I am grateful for the opportunities I have been given to do so.

This book is not just mine—it belongs to all of you who have walked alongside me, supported me, and believed in the power of kindness, authenticity, and purpose. Thank you for being a part of my journey.

ABOUT JO ANN

JO ANN HEROLD is a purpose-driven marketing leader, brand strategist, and author known for her leadership with iconic brands. She currently serves as the Vice President of Marketing at Georgia State University, where she leads the institution's marketing strategy, brand positioning, and engagement efforts.

Herold is also the author of the best-selling memoir, *Living on a Smile: 16 Ways to Live a Big Life and Lead with Love*, a book that shares insights on leadership, personal growth, and purpose.

Prior to her role at Georgia State, Herold held high-profile marketing leadership positions, including Chief Marketing Officer at The Honey Baked Ham Company (twice), Global Chief Marketing Office at Interface, Inc. and Vice President of Brand and Communications at Arby's Restaurant Group. In all of these roles, she played a crucial part in brand transformations, sustainability, and growth strategies.

In addition to these roles, Herold is on the Executive Board of *Fast Company* and is a frequent contributor, sharing her expertise on branding and leadership. She has received numerous industry awards recognizing her contributions to marketing and leadership, including several Effies, a personal Lifetime Achievement from the Atlanta American Marketing Association, and the Marketer for Good.

Herold is known for her ability to drive business growth while fostering a culture of teamwork, authenticity, and kindness in the workplace. She loves family, walking in Atlanta and all over the world, concerts, and being with family and friends.